The Teenage Mind: A Guide To Understanding And Navigating The Complex World Of Adolescents

Negoita Manuela

Published by Negoita Manuela, 2024.

While every precaution has been taken in the preparation of this book, the publisher assumes no responsibility for errors or omissions, or for damages resulting from the use of the information contained herein.

THE TEENAGE MIND: A GUIDE TO UNDERSTANDING AND NAVIGATING THE COMPLEX WORLD OF ADOLESCENTS

First edition. March 31, 2024.

ISBN: 979-8224719266

Written by Negoita Manuela.

Table of Contents

Chapter 1: Introduction

- THE DEFINITION OF adolescence

Adolescence is a critical stage in human development that spans the period between childhood and adulthood. It is characterized by rapid physical, emotional, and cognitive changes that shape an individual's identity and set the foundation for their future growth and success. This stage typically begins around the age of 10 or 11 and continues until the late teens or early twenties, depending on cultural and societal norms.

During adolescence, young people experience significant physical changes as they enter puberty and undergo sexual maturation. These changes include growth spurts, the development of secondary sexual characteristics such as breasts and facial hair, and the onset of menstruation in girls. Hormonal fluctuations play a key role in these transformations, affecting mood, energy levels, and sexual desire. It is important for adolescents to receive accurate information about their changing bodies and to have access to healthcare services to address any concerns or issues that may arise during this time.

In addition to physical development, adolescents also experience profound emotional and cognitive changes that shape their sense of self and relationships with others. This period is marked by a heightened level of self-awareness and a desire for independence from parents and other authority figures. Adolescents may experiment with different identities, beliefs, and values as they seek to forge their own path in the world. This can lead to conflicts with parents and peers as they navigate the complex terrain of social relationships and personal boundaries.

Cognitive development during adolescence is also significant, with young people gaining the ability to think abstractly and critically about themselves and the world around them. They become more capable of forming their own opinions, making decisions, and planning for the future. However, this newfound cognitive ability is often accompanied by a sense of vulnerability and uncertainty as adolescents grapple with the complexities of adulthood and the responsibilities that come with it.

One of the key challenges of adolescence is the transition from dependence on parents to autonomy and self-sufficiency. This process, known as individuation, involves establishing a sense of personal identity separate from one's family and developing the skills and resources to navigate the world independently. This can be a tumultuous time for both adolescents and their parents, as they negotiate boundaries, rules, and responsibilities in a way that allows the young person to develop a sense of self-efficacy and agency. It is a time of exploration, growth, and self-discovery, as young people navigate the challenges of identity formation, independence, and decision-making. By understanding the unique needs and experiences of adolescents, we can better support them in their journey toward becoming healthy, resilient, and successful adults.

- The challenges faced by teenagers

Teenagers face a myriad of challenges as they navigate the transition from childhood to adulthood. One of the most significant challenges they encounter is peer pressure. Adolescents are often influenced by their peers to engage in risky behaviors such as drug and alcohol use, smoking, and unsafe sexual practices. This pressure to conform to the norms of their social group can be overwhelming and can lead to long-term negative consequences. It is important for teenagers to develop strong self-esteem and assertiveness skills to resist peer pressure and make healthy choices for themselves.

Another challenge faced by teenagers is academic pressure. As they progress through high school, teenagers are often faced with increasing academic demands, such as exams, projects, and college applications. The pressure to excel academically can be intense and can lead to stress, anxiety, and burnout. It is important for teenagers to learn how to manage their time effectively, seek help when needed, and practice self-care to maintain their mental and emotional well-being.

Social media and technology also present unique challenges for teenagers. With the rise of social media platforms such as Instagram, Snapchat, and TikTok, teenagers are constantly exposed to unrealistic beauty standards, cyberbullying, and the pressure to present a curated version of their lives online. This can lead to feelings of inadequacy, anxiety, and isolation. It is crucial for teenagers to develop healthy digital habits, set boundaries for themselves, and seek support from trusted adults if they are experiencing negative effects from their online interactions.

Mental health issues are also a significant challenge for teenagers. Adolescence is a period of rapid physical, emotional, and cognitive development, and teenagers are vulnerable to mood swings, anxiety, depression, and other mental health conditions. Stigma and lack of awareness surrounding mental health can prevent teenagers from seeking help when they need it. It is important for parents, educators, and healthcare providers to destigmatize mental health issues, provide resources and support for teenagers, and promote open communication about mental health.

Identity and self-discovery are central themes of adolescence, and teenagers often struggle to form their own sense of identity in the midst of societal expectations, peer pressure, and family dynamics. Questions of sexuality, gender identity, and cultural heritage can be particularly challenging for teenagers to navigate. It is essential for teenagers to have opportunities for self-expression, exploration, and reflection to develop a strong sense of self and build healthy relationships with others. From peer pressure and academic stress to social media influence and mental health issues, adolescents must develop resilience, self-awareness, and coping strategies to thrive during this transformative period of their lives. It is essential for parents, educators, healthcare providers, and society as a whole to support teenagers, provide resources and guidance, and create a safe and nurturing environment for them to explore their identities, build healthy relationships, and achieve their full potential. By addressing the unique challenges faced by teenagers with empathy, understanding, and support, we can help them navigate this critical stage of development and emerge as confident, capable, and resilient young adults.

- The importance of understanding the teenage mind

The teenage years are a pivotal and transformative period in an individual's life. During this time, adolescents undergo significant physical, emotional, and cognitive changes as they navigate the transition from childhood to adulthood. It is crucial for parents, educators, and mental health professionals to understand the complexities of the teenage mind in order to provide appropriate support and guidance during this critical stage of development.

One of the key reasons why understanding the teenage mind is so important is that adolescents are highly vulnerable to mental health issues. Research has shown that many mental health disorders, such as depression, anxiety, and eating disorders, often first emerge during adolescence. This can be attributed to the intense pressures and challenges that teenagers face, including academic stress, social pressures, and hormonal changes. By gaining insight into the unique psychological and emotional needs of teenagers, parents and educators can better identify warning signs of mental health issues and intervene early to prevent more serious consequences.

In addition to mental health concerns, understanding the teenage mind is crucial for fostering positive relationships and communication between adolescents and adults. Teenagers often struggle with expressing their thoughts and emotions, which can lead to misunderstandings and conflicts with parents, teachers, and peers. By taking the time to listen to teenagers and validate their experiences, adults can build trust and open lines of communication that are essential for supporting teenagers through the challenges of adolescence. This can help teenagers feel understood, valued, and supported, which can ultimately improve their overall well-being and mental health.

Furthermore, understanding the teenage mind is important for promoting healthy decision-making and risk-taking behaviors. Adolescents are biologically predisposed to seek out new experiences and take risks, which can sometimes lead to impulsive and dangerous behaviors. By understanding the neurobiology of the teenage brain and how it influences decision-making, parents and educators can help teenagers develop their executive functioning skills and make more informed choices. This can empower teenagers to navigate challenging situations, such as peer pressure, substance use, and risky behaviors, in a safe and responsible manner.

Another reason why understanding the teenage mind is essential is that it can help adults support teenagers in developing their sense of identity and self-esteem. Adolescence is a time of exploration and self-discovery, during which teenagers are grappling with questions of who they are, what they believe, and where they fit in the world. By listening to teenagers' perspectives and validating their feelings, adults can help adolescents develop a strong sense of self and confidence in their own identities. This can help teenagers navigate the complexities of adolescence with resilience and self-assurance, laying the foundation for healthy adult relationships and personal fulfillment. By recognizing the unique challenges and vulnerabilities that teenagers face, adults can provide support, guidance, and mentorship that empowers teenagers to navigate the complexities of adolescence with confidence and resilience. By fostering positive relationships, open communication, and healthy decision-making skills, adults can help teenagers thrive and reach their full potential as they transition into adulthood. Ultimately, by investing in understanding and supporting the teenage mind, we can create a more compassionate and nurturing environment for the next generation of young people.

Chapter 2: The Science of Adolescent Brain Development

- HOW THE TEENAGE BRAIN is different from an adult brain

The teenage brain is a complex and fascinating organ that undergoes significant changes during the adolescent years. One of the key differences between the teenage brain and the adult brain is in its development and maturation. The teenage brain is still in the process of developing and refining its neural circuits, which are responsible for critical thinking, decision making, and emotional regulation. This period of development, known as neuroplasticity, allows the brain to adapt and change in response to experiences and environments.

One of the most significant differences between the teenage brain and the adult brain is the prefrontal cortex, which is responsible for higher-order cognitive functions such as decision making, impulse control, and planning. In teenagers, the prefrontal cortex is still developing and may not reach full maturity until the mid-20s. This means that teenagers may struggle with making decisions, regulating their emotions, and controlling their impulses more than adults. This can lead to risky behavior, impulsivity, and poor decision making during the teenage years.

Another key difference between the teenage brain and the adult brain is in the way that they process emotions. The limbic system, which is responsible for processing emotions, is more active in teenagers than in adults. This can lead to heightened emotional responses, increased mood swings, and greater vulnerability to stress and anxiety. Additionally, the connections between the limbic system and the prefrontal cortex are still developing during adolescence, which can further contribute to emotional volatility and impulsivity in teenagers.

The teenage brain also undergoes changes in the way that it responds to rewards and risks. The reward system in the brain, which is centered in the nucleus accumbens, is more sensitive in teenagers than in adults. This means that teenagers are more likely to seek out rewarding experiences and take risks in order to achieve those rewards. This can lead to risky behavior, such as substance abuse, reckless driving, and unprotected sex, as teenagers are more likely to focus on the potential rewards of these behaviors without fully considering the risks.

In addition to these differences in brain development, there are also structural differences between the teenage brain and the adult brain. For example, the amount of white matter in the brain, which is responsible for communication between different regions of the brain, increases during adolescence and peaks in early adulthood. This increase in white matter allows for more efficient communication and processing of information in the brain. However, the development of white matter in the brain is not uniform across all regions, which can lead to imbalances in communication and coordination between different regions of the brain in teenagers.

Despite these differences in brain development, it is important to note that the teenage brain is not inherently flawed or deficient compared to the adult brain. The changes that occur during adolescence are a normal part of brain development and are essential for preparing teenagers for adulthood. Furthermore, the plasticity of the teenage brain means that it is highly adaptable and responsive to changes in the environment. With the right support, guidance, and opportunities for growth, teenagers can develop strong cognitive and emotional skills that will serve them well throughout their lives. These differences can manifest in behaviors such as impulsivity, emotional volatility, and risk-taking during adolescence. However, it is important to recognize that these differences are a normal part of brain development and are essential for preparing teenagers for adulthood. With the right support and guidance, teenagers can navigate the challenges of adolescence and emerge as resilient, capable adults.

- The impact of hormones on behavior

Hormones are chemical messengers that play a crucial role in regulating various physiological processes in the human body, including growth, metabolism, and reproduction. In addition to their role in controlling bodily functions, hormones also have a significant impact on behavior. The complex interplay between hormones and behavior is a fascinating area of study that has captured the interest of researchers across disciplines, from psychology and neuroscience to endocrinology and genetics.

One of the key ways in which hormones influence behavior is through their effects on mood and emotional responses. For example, the hormone cortisol, which is released in response to stress, can have a profound impact on an individual's emotional state. High levels of cortisol have been linked to feelings of anxiety and depression, while low levels have been associated with improved mood and overall well-being. Similarly, the hormone oxytocin, often referred to as the "love hormone," plays a crucial role in social bonding and attachment. Studies have shown that individuals with higher levels of oxytocin tend to have stronger social connections and more positive relationships with others.

In addition to their effects on mood and emotions, hormones also play a key role in regulating aggression and other forms of social behavior. Testosterone, a hormone primarily produced in males but also present in females in smaller amounts, has long been associated with aggressive behavior. Studies have shown that individuals with higher levels of testosterone are more likely to exhibit dominance and competitiveness, traits that are often linked to aggression. However, it is important to note that the relationship between testosterone and aggression is complex and influenced by a variety of factors, including individual differences, social context, and cultural norms.

Beyond their effects on mood, emotions, and social behavior, hormones also influence cognitive processes such as memory, learning, and decision-making. For example, the hormone estrogen has been shown to play a role in enhancing cognitive function, particularly in areas related to verbal memory and spatial navigation. Studies have also suggested that estrogen may have a protective effect against age-related cognitive decline and neurodegenerative diseases such as Alzheimer's. Similarly, the hormone insulin, which is central to regulating blood sugar levels, has been found to impact cognitive function by influencing brain energy metabolism and neurotransmitter function.

The impact of hormones on behavior is not limited to individual differences but also extends to broader societal issues such as gender identity and sexual orientation. Hormones play a critical role in the development of sexual characteristics and behaviors, influencing everything from physical appearance to sexual orientation. For example, the hormone testosterone is responsible for the development of male secondary sexual characteristics such as facial hair and deep voice, as well as the expression of male-typical behaviors. In contrast, the hormone estrogen plays a key role in the development of female secondary sexual characteristics such as breast development and menstrual cycles, as well as the expression of female-typical behaviors. The complex interplay between hormones and behavior underscores the importance of a holistic approach to understanding human behavior, one that takes into account the intricate network of biological, psychological, and social factors that influence our thoughts, feelings, and actions. By further investigating the impact of hormones on behavior, researchers can gain valuable insights into the underlying mechanisms that drive human behavior and mental health, ultimately leading to more effective interventions and treatments for a variety of behavioral and psychiatric disorders.

- The development of decision-making skills

Decision-making is a crucial aspect of everyday life. It is the process of selecting a course of action from multiple options, based on careful consideration of various factors. The ability to make sound decisions is a skill that is essential for personal and professional success. Therefore, the development of decision-making skills is a topic that has garnered much attention in academic circles.

According to research in the field of psychology, decision-making is a complex cognitive process that involves weighing the pros and cons of different options, considering the potential outcomes, and selecting the best course of action. It is influenced by a variety of factors, including the individual's values, beliefs, emotions, and past experiences. As such, developing effective decision-making skills requires a combination of knowledge, critical thinking, and self-awareness.

One of the key components of improving decision-making skills is understanding the decision-making process itself. By breaking down the process into its constituent parts, individuals can gain a better understanding of how decisions are made and what factors influence them. For example, the recognition of alternative options, the evaluation of potential outcomes, and the selection of the best course of action are all important steps in the decision-making process. By understanding these steps, individuals can improve their ability to make informed and rational decisions.

Another important aspect of developing decision-making skills is the ability to gather and analyze information. Making decisions without sufficient information can lead to poor outcomes, so it is important to take the time to gather relevant data and evaluate it critically. This may involve conducting research, consulting with experts, or seeking out different perspectives. By taking a systematic approach to information gathering and analysis, individuals can make more informed decisions that are based on evidence rather than gut feelings.

In addition to gathering information, it is also crucial to consider the potential risks and benefits of different options when making a decision. Risk assessment involves identifying potential pitfalls and weighing them against potential rewards. By carefully considering the risks and benefits of each option, individuals can make decisions that are more likely to lead to positive outcomes. This also involves considering the long-term consequences of decisions and how they may impact future goals and objectives.

Emotional intelligence is also an important factor in the development of decision-making skills. Emotions can play a significant role in the decision-making process, as they can influence how individuals perceive and evaluate different options. By developing emotional intelligence, individuals can become more aware of their emotions and how they may be influencing their decisions. This can help individuals to make more rational and objective decisions that are based on logic rather than emotions.

Furthermore, developing decision-making skills also involves developing critical thinking skills. Critical thinking is the ability to evaluate information, identify underlying assumptions, and draw logical conclusions. By honing their critical thinking skills, individuals can become more adept at analyzing complex problems and making sound decisions. This may involve questioning assumptions, considering alternative viewpoints, and challenging their own beliefs. By developing critical thinking skills, individuals can make more informed and effective decisions in a wide range of situations. By understanding the decision-making process, gathering and analyzing information, assessing the risks and benefits of different options, and developing emotional intelligence and critical thinking skills, individuals can improve their ability to make informed and rational decisions. Ultimately, the development of decision-making skills is essential for personal and professional success, as it enables individuals to navigate complex situations and make choices that lead to positive outcomes.

Chapter 3: Emotional Development in Adolescence

- THE ROLE OF EMOTIONS in teenage behavior

The teenage years are a period of rapid physical, emotional, and cognitive development. During this time, adolescents are beginning to form their own identity, establish independence from their families, and navigate the complexities of social relationships. Emotions play a crucial role in shaping teenage behavior, influencing how they think, feel, and act in various situations.

One of the key functions of emotions in teenage behavior is to help adolescents respond to and make sense of their environment. Emotions serve as powerful signals that alert teenagers to potential threats or rewards in their surroundings, guiding their decisions and actions. For example, feelings of fear can prompt a teenager to avoid a potentially dangerous situation, while feelings of excitement can motivate them to pursue a rewarding opportunity. By experiencing and expressing emotions, teenagers are able to adapt to changing social and environmental demands, learn from their experiences, and develop important coping skills.

In addition to helping teenagers navigate their world, emotions also play a critical role in forming and maintaining relationships with others. Adolescents are increasingly attuned to the emotions of their peers and are learning how to empathize with others, communicate their own feelings, and regulate their emotional responses in social interactions. For example, teenagers who are able to accurately perceive and respond to the emotions of their friends are more likely to have positive and satisfying friendships. Conversely, teenagers who struggle with regulating their emotions may have difficulty forming and maintaining relationships, leading to feelings of loneliness and isolation.

Furthermore, emotions can influence teenage behavior in both positive and negative ways. On the positive side, emotions such as empathy, compassion, and gratitude can promote prosocial behaviors, such as helping others, sharing resources, and cooperating with peers. These emotions help teenagers build strong and supportive relationships, develop a sense of moral identity, and contribute to the well-being of their communities. On the other hand, negative emotions, such as anger, jealousy, and sadness, can contribute to aggressive or antisocial behaviors, such as bullying, vandalism, and substance abuse. These emotions may arise from stressful or challenging situations, and if left unaddressed, can lead to harmful and destructive behavior.

It is important for parents, teachers, and other caregivers to help teenagers recognize, understand, and manage their emotions in healthy and productive ways. By fostering emotional intelligence, which involves being aware of one's own emotions, understanding the emotions of others, and effectively regulating emotions, adults can support teenagers in making informed decisions, forming positive relationships, and coping with the challenges of adolescence. Adults can also help teenagers develop effective strategies for managing stress, such as engaging in physical activity, practicing mindfulness, seeking social support, and engaging in creative outlets. By modeling healthy emotional expression and communication, adults can empower teenagers to navigate their emotions, make responsible choices, and thrive in all aspects of their lives. Emotions serve as important signals that guide teenagers in navigating their environment, forming relationships with others, and making decisions. By understanding and managing their emotions in healthy ways, teenagers can develop important skills for coping with the challenges of adolescence, building positive relationships, and contributing to their communities. By supporting teenagers in developing emotional intelligence, adults can empower them to thrive and succeed in all aspects of their lives.

- **Common emotional challenges faced by teenagers**

Teenagers often face a plethora of emotional challenges as they navigate the tumultuous waters of adolescence. These challenges can stem from a variety of sources, including hormonal changes, peer pressure, academic stress, family dynamics, and societal expectations. It is not uncommon for teenagers to experience feelings of anxiety, depression, loneliness, anger, and confusion as they try to establish their identity and place in the world.

One of the most common emotional challenges faced by teenagers is the pressure to perform well academically. As students are expected to excel in school in order to secure a successful future, many teenagers experience overwhelming stress and anxiety related to their academic performance. This pressure can manifest in various ways, such as fear of failure, perfectionism, and feelings of inadequacy. Teenagers may also struggle with time management and balancing competing demands, leading to feelings of overwhelm and burnout.

In addition to academic stress, teenagers often grapple with the complexities of their interpersonal relationships. Peer pressure, social media, and societal norms can all contribute to feelings of insecurity, loneliness, and alienation. Teenagers may feel intense pressure to fit in and conform to societal expectations, which can lead to emotional distress and feelings of inadequacy. Bullying, cyberbullying, and peer rejection are also common challenges that teenagers face, which can further exacerbate feelings of isolation and self-doubt.

Family dynamics can also play a significant role in the emotional challenges that teenagers face. Conflict with parents, siblings, and other family members can create tension and stress within the household, leading to feelings of frustration, anger, and resentment. Teenagers may struggle to assert their independence and autonomy while also seeking approval and validation from their family members, which can create a sense of internal conflict and emotional turmoil. Communication breakdowns and lack of understanding between family members can further complicate these relationships and contribute to emotional distress.

Moreover, the rapid physical and hormonal changes that occur during adolescence can have a profound impact on teenagers' emotional well-being. Hormonal fluctuations can lead to mood swings, irritability, and intense emotions, which can be difficult for teenagers to manage and regulate. The physical changes that accompany puberty, such as changes in body shape, acne, and growth spurts, can also trigger feelings of insecurity and self-consciousness, which can affect teenagers' self-esteem and body image. Academic stress, peer pressure, family dynamics, and hormonal changes can all contribute to feelings of anxiety, depression, loneliness, and confusion. It is important for teenagers to receive support and guidance from trusted adults, such as parents, teachers, and mental health professionals, in order to navigate these challenges and build resilience. By fostering open communication, providing a supportive environment, and encouraging self-care and self-compassion, we can help teenagers navigate the emotional challenges of adolescence and emerge stronger and more resilient on the other side.

- Effective ways to cope with emotional turmoil

Emotional turmoil is a common experience that many individuals face at some point in their lives. It can be caused by a variety of factors such as relationship issues, work stress, financial problems, or health concerns. Coping with emotional turmoil is essential in order to maintain mental health and overall well-being. There are several effective ways to cope with emotional turmoil that can help individuals navigate difficult emotions and emerge stronger on the other side.

One effective way to cope with emotional turmoil is to practice mindfulness and meditation. Mindfulness involves being fully present in the moment and observing your thoughts and feelings without judgment. Meditation can help calm the mind and reduce stress, allowing individuals to gain a sense of clarity and perspective on their emotions. By incorporating mindfulness and meditation into your daily routine, you can learn to manage your emotions more effectively and cope with emotional turmoil in a healthier way.

Another effective way to cope with emotional turmoil is to engage in self-care activities that nurture your mind, body, and soul. Taking care of yourself is crucial during times of emotional distress, as self-care can help replenish your energy and boost your mood. This can involve activities such as exercising, getting enough sleep, eating a nutritious diet, spending time in nature, or engaging in hobbies that bring you joy. By prioritizing self-care, you can build resilience and better cope with the challenges that come your way.

Seeking support from friends, family, or a therapist can also be instrumental in coping with emotional turmoil. Talking about your feelings with a trusted confidante can provide a sense of relief and validation, as well as help you gain new insights into your emotions. A therapist can offer professional guidance and support, helping you develop coping strategies and navigate difficult emotions in a healthy way. Building a support network of caring individuals can provide a strong foundation for coping with emotional turmoil and fostering emotional resilience.

In addition to these strategies, practicing self-compassion and acceptance can be powerful tools for coping with emotional turmoil. Self-compassion involves treating yourself with kindness and understanding, especially during times of distress. By acknowledging your feelings without judgment and showing yourself empathy, you can cultivate a sense of inner strength and resilience. Acceptance involves facing difficult emotions head-on and allowing yourself to feel them fully, without trying to suppress or avoid them. By embracing your emotions with acceptance, you can move through them in a healthy way and find greater peace and clarity.

It is important to remember that coping with emotional turmoil is a process that takes time and patience. It is normal to experience a range of emotions during difficult times, and it is important to be gentle with yourself as you navigate these feelings. By incorporating mindfulness, self-care, support, self-compassion, and acceptance into your coping strategies, you can build emotional resilience and find healthy ways to cope with emotional turmoil. Remember that you are not alone in facing emotional challenges, and that there are resources and support available to help you navigate difficult emotions and emerge stronger on the other side.

Chapter 4: Social Influences on Teenage Behavior

- THE IMPACT OF PEER pressure on decision-making

Peer pressure can have a significant impact on decision-making, especially during adolescence when individuals are most susceptible to the influence of their peers. Research has shown that peer pressure can lead individuals to make decisions that they would not have made on their own, whether it be positive or negative. Peer pressure can come in various forms, such as direct peer pressure, indirect peer pressure, and even self-induced peer pressure. Understanding the dynamics of peer pressure and its impact on decision-making is crucial in order to develop effective strategies to resist negative influences and make informed decisions.

One of the key factors contributing to the impact of peer pressure on decision-making is the desire to fit in and be accepted by one's peers. Adolescents are at a stage in their development where social acceptance plays a significant role in their identity formation. As a result, they may be more likely to conform to the behavior of their peers in order to gain acceptance and avoid social rejection. This desire to fit in can override their own values and beliefs, leading them to make decisions that may not align with their own moral compass.

Another factor that contributes to the impact of peer pressure on decision-making is the fear of missing out or being left out. Adolescents often fear being excluded from social activities or being seen as different from their peers. This fear can drive them to make decisions based on what they perceive to be the norm among their peer group, rather than what they truly want or believe is right. This fear of missing out can lead individuals to engage in risky behaviors or make impulsive decisions in order to avoid being left out or ostracized by their peers.

In addition to the desire to fit in and the fear of missing out, peer pressure can also influence decision-making through the process of social comparison. Adolescents may compare themselves to their peers in terms of appearance, academic performance, social status, and other aspects of their lives. This constant comparison can lead individuals to make decisions based on what they believe will make them more similar to their peers or help them to achieve a higher social status. This can result in individuals making decisions that are not in their best interest or that may have negative consequences in the long run.

While peer pressure can have a negative impact on decision-making, it is important to note that it can also have positive effects. Peers can encourage each other to engage in healthy behaviors, such as exercising, eating well, and studying hard. Positive peer pressure can provide individuals with a sense of support and motivation to make positive choices and pursue their goals. However, it is essential for individuals to be able to distinguish between positive and negative peer pressure in order to make informed decisions that align with their values and goals.

In order to resist negative peer pressure and make informed decisions, individuals can develop strategies to strengthen their ability to think critically and independently. This may involve building self-confidence, assertiveness, and communication skills in order to resist peer pressure and assert one's own values and beliefs. It may also involve surrounding oneself with positive influences and supportive peers who encourage healthy behaviors and respect individual differences. Additionally, individuals can practice mindfulness and reflection to better understand their own motivations and values, and to make decisions that are in alignment with their long-term goals and well-being. Understanding the dynamics of peer pressure and its effects on decision-making is crucial in order to develop strategies to resist negative influences and make informed choices. By building self-confidence, assertiveness, and critical thinking skills, individuals can resist negative peer pressure and make decisions that align with their values and goals. Positive peer pressure can also have a beneficial impact on decision-making, encouraging individuals to engage in healthy behaviors and pursue their goals.

- The importance of social connections in adolescence

Adolescence is a critical period of development during which individuals undergo significant physical, emotional, and cognitive changes. It is a time of exploration, self-discovery, and identity formation. One key aspect of adolescent development that is often overlooked is the importance of social connections. Social connections refer to the relationships that adolescents have with their peers, family members, teachers, and other adults in their lives. These relationships play a crucial role in shaping adolescents' social skills, emotional well-being, and overall development.

Social connections are important for several reasons. First and foremost, they provide adolescents with a sense of belonging and acceptance. During adolescence, individuals begin to form their own identity separate from their families. Having positive relationships with peers and adults outside of the family can help adolescents feel accepted and valued. This sense of belonging is essential for building self-esteem and confidence, which are important for navigating the challenges of adolescence.

Furthermore, social connections provide adolescents with emotional support. Adolescence is a time of heightened emotional intensity, as individuals grapple with issues such as peer pressure, academic stress, and identity confusion. Having a strong support network can help adolescents cope with these challenges and develop healthy coping mechanisms. Research has shown that individuals who have strong social connections are less likely to experience depression, anxiety, and other mental health issues.

In addition to providing emotional support, social connections also play a key role in shaping adolescents' social skills. Through interactions with peers and adults, adolescents learn how to communicate effectively, resolve conflicts, and navigate social situations. These social skills are crucial for building relationships, succeeding in school and later in life, and forming a strong support network. Adolescents who have positive social connections are more likely to have successful interpersonal relationships and thrive in various social settings.

Furthermore, social connections can have a profound impact on adolescents' academic success. Research has shown that students who have strong relationships with teachers and peers are more engaged in school, achieve higher grades, and are more likely to graduate. Teachers and peers can provide academic support, encouragement, and motivation, which are essential for academic success. Additionally, having positive social connections can enhance adolescents' sense of belonging and connectedness to their school community, which can lead to greater academic achievement.

It is important to note that social connections are not limited to peers and adults outside of the family. Family relationships also play a crucial role in shaping adolescents' social development. Research has shown that adolescents who have strong relationships with their families are more likely to have positive social connections with peers and adults outside of the family. Family relationships provide a secure base from which adolescents can explore and develop their social skills. They also serve as a source of support, guidance, and love, which are essential for adolescents' overall well-being. They provide adolescents with a sense of belonging, emotional support, social skills, and academic success. Building positive relationships with peers, family members, teachers, and other adults is essential for adolescents to navigate the challenges of adolescence, develop healthy coping mechanisms, and thrive in various social settings. As educators, parents, and policymakers, it is important to recognize the importance of social connections and provide adolescents with opportunities to build and maintain positive relationships. By fostering strong social connections, we can help adolescents reach their full potential and lead healthy, fulfilling lives.

- How to navigate social relationships in a healthy way

Navigating social relationships in a healthy way is a crucial aspect of our daily lives. Whether it be with colleagues, friends, family members, or romantic partners, the quality of our relationships can greatly impact our overall well-being and mental health. However, fostering healthy relationships can sometimes be challenging, as it requires effective communication, emotional intelligence, and a willingness to work through conflicts and misunderstandings. In this essay, we will explore some key strategies and tips for navigating social relationships in a healthy and constructive manner.

One of the most important aspects of navigating social relationships in a healthy way is effective communication. Communication is the foundation of any relationship, and being able to express our thoughts, feelings, and needs clearly and respectfully is essential for building strong and meaningful connections with others. It is important to actively listen to others, show empathy and understanding, and be open and honest in our own communication. Avoiding passive-aggressive behavior and being willing to address conflicts and issues directly can help prevent misunderstandings and build trust in the relationship.

Emotional intelligence is another key component of navigating social relationships in a healthy way. Emotional intelligence involves being aware of our own emotions and the emotions of others, and being able to manage these emotions effectively in social interactions. Developing emotional intelligence can help us respond to others in a more empathetic and understanding way, and can prevent misunderstandings and conflicts from escalating. Practicing self-awareness, self-regulation, and empathy can help us build stronger and more resilient relationships with others.

Setting boundaries is also important for navigating social relationships in a healthy way. Boundaries help us define our own needs, values, and limits, and communicate these to others in a clear and respectful manner. Setting boundaries can help prevent us from feeling overwhelmed or taken advantage of in relationships, and can ensure that our needs are respected and met. It is important to communicate our boundaries assertively and without guilt, and to be willing to enforce them when necessary. Respect for boundaries is essential for maintaining healthy and respectful relationships with others.

Conflict resolution is another crucial skill for navigating social relationships in a healthy way. Conflict is a natural part of any relationship, and being able to address and resolve conflicts constructively is essential for maintaining strong and healthy connections with others. It is important to approach conflicts with an open mind and a willingness to listen to the perspectives of others, and to seek mutually beneficial solutions to problems. Avoiding blame, criticism, and defensiveness, and instead focusing on understanding and finding common ground, can help prevent conflicts from escalating and damaging the relationship.

Building trust is essential for navigating social relationships in a healthy way. Trust is the foundation of any relationship, and without trust, it can be difficult to establish open and honest communication, mutual respect, and emotional intimacy with others. Building trust takes time and effort, but it is crucial for fostering strong and meaningful connections with others. It is important to be reliable, consistent, and authentic in our interactions with others, and to show respect and consideration for their feelings and needs. Trust is the basis for a healthy and fulfilling relationship.

All in all, self-care is essential for navigating social relationships in a healthy way. Taking care of our own physical, emotional, and mental well-being is crucial for being able to show up fully in our relationships with others. It is important to prioritize self-care activities that recharge and refresh us, such as exercise, meditation, hobbies, and spending time with loved ones. Taking care of ourselves allows us to show up as our best selves in our relationships, and to approach others with empathy, patience, and understanding. Self-care is a crucial aspect of maintaining healthy and fulfilling relationships with others. By cultivating these skills and strategies, we can foster strong and meaningful connections with others, and build relationships that are fulfilling, supportive, and enriching. It is important to approach relationships with an open mind and a willingness to learn and grow, and to prioritize mutual respect, empathy, and understanding in our interactions with others. By investing time and effort into developing healthy relationships, we can create a positive and supportive social network that enhances our overall well-being and satisfaction in life.

Chapter 5: Identity Formation in Adolescence

- THE SEARCH FOR SELF-identity in teenagers

The search for self-identity in teenagers is a complex and nuanced process that is influenced by various internal and external factors. Adolescence is a critical period in an individual's development where they begin to question their identity, values, and beliefs. During this time, teenagers are exploring different aspects of themselves, such as their interests, talents, and passions, in order to form a coherent sense of self. This search for self-identity can be both exhilarating and daunting as teenagers navigate the challenges of adolescence while trying to define who they are as individuals.

One of the key factors that influences the search for self-identity in teenagers is the role of social relationships. Adolescents are heavily influenced by their peers, family members, and cultural environment, which can shape their sense of self. Peer groups play a significant role in the formation of identity as teenagers seek acceptance and validation from their peers. This can lead to conformity and pressure to fit in with the group, which can hinder the exploration of one's true self. On the other hand, positive relationships with family members and mentors can provide support and encouragement for teenagers to explore their interests and values, helping them to develop a strong sense of self-identity.

Another important factor that influences the search for self-identity in teenagers is the impact of social media and technology. In today's digital age, teenagers are constantly exposed to a barrage of images and messages that can shape their self-perception. Social media platforms provide a platform for teenagers to showcase their lives and project a certain image of themselves to the world. This pressure to maintain a curated online persona can lead to feelings of inadequacy and comparison with others, making it difficult for teenagers to find their authentic self. It is important for teenagers to critically evaluate the influence of social media on their self-identity and to focus on building genuine connections with others offline.

Cultural and societal expectations also play a significant role in shaping the search for self-identity in teenagers. Adolescents may feel pressure to conform to certain gender roles, cultural norms, or societal expectations, which can impact their sense of self. For example, teenagers from minority cultural backgrounds may struggle to balance their cultural identity with the pressure to assimilate into the dominant culture. This conflict can create internal struggles and identity crises for teenagers as they try to navigate their multiple identities. It is important for teenagers to feel free to explore and express their unique identity without fear of judgment or discrimination based on societal norms.

The search for self-identity in teenagers can also be influenced by individual factors, such as personality traits, values, and interests. Each teenager is unique and has their own set of strengths, weaknesses, and characteristics that define who they are. Some teenagers may have a clear sense of self from an early age, while others may struggle to define their identity well into adulthood. Personality traits, such as introversion or extroversion, can influence how teenagers perceive themselves and interact with others. Values and interests, such as a passion for the arts or social justice, can shape teenagers' sense of purpose and direction in life. It is important for teenagers to explore their individuality and embrace their unique qualities in order to develop a strong sense of self-identity. Adolescents navigate the complexities of adolescence as they explore different aspects of themselves, seek validation from peers, and reconcile cultural and societal expectations. It is important for teenagers to critically evaluate the influences on their self-identity and to cultivate a strong sense of self that is authentic and true to who they are. By exploring their interests, values, and personality traits, teenagers can develop a coherent sense of identity that serves as a foundation for their growth and development into adulthood.

- The role of self-esteem and self-concept

Self-esteem and self-concept play significant roles in shaping an individual's perception of themselves and their interactions with others. Self-esteem refers to the overall sense of self-worth and value that a person possesses, while self-concept encompasses the beliefs and attitudes that an individual holds about themselves. These two aspects of self-perception are closely related and can greatly influence a person's mental and emotional well-being.

One of the key components of self-esteem is self-evaluation, which involves assessing one's own abilities, characteristics, and behaviors. When individuals have a positive self-esteem, they tend to have a high regard for themselves and believe in their own capabilities. This confidence in oneself can lead to success in various aspects of life, such as relationships, career, and personal development. On the other hand, individuals with low self-esteem may struggle with feelings of inadequacy, self-doubt, and insecurity, which can impact their overall happiness and quality of life.

Self-concept, on the other hand, refers to the beliefs and attitudes that individuals hold about themselves in relation to their experiences, abilities, and characteristics. These beliefs can be influenced by various factors, such as social interactions, cultural norms, and personal achievements. A positive self-concept involves having a realistic and balanced view of oneself, acknowledging strengths and weaknesses while still maintaining a sense of self-worth. In contrast, a negative self-concept can lead to feelings of self-criticism, self-doubt, and low self-esteem.

It is important to note that self-esteem and self-concept are not fixed traits, but rather dynamic aspects of a person's identity that can change over time. Factors such as life experiences, relationships, and personal growth can all contribute to shaping and influencing an individual's self-esteem and self-concept. For example, positive feedback and validation from others can boost a person's self-esteem, while negative experiences or criticism can damage it. Similarly, personal achievements and successes can enhance one's self-concept, while failures and setbacks can challenge it.

The relationship between self-esteem and self-concept is complex and multifaceted. While self-esteem is more focused on overall feelings of self-worth and value, self-concept delves deeper into specific beliefs and attitudes that individuals hold about themselves. However, the two are closely intertwined, as self-esteem can influence self-concept and vice versa. For example, individuals with a high self-esteem may have a more positive self-concept, as they are more likely to view themselves in a favorable light and focus on their strengths and abilities. Conversely, those with low self-esteem may have a negative self-concept, as they may struggle to see themselves in a positive way and may be more critical of their flaws and shortcomings.

It is also important to recognize that self-esteem and self-concept can have a profound impact on various aspects of an individual's life, including relationships, career, and personal well-being. For example, individuals with high self-esteem and a positive self-concept are more likely to have healthy and fulfilling relationships, as they are better able to communicate their needs, set boundaries, and assert themselves in a positive way. On the other hand, those with low self-esteem and a negative self-concept may have difficulty forming meaningful connections with others, as they may struggle with feelings of inadequacy and self-doubt.

In terms of career and personal development, self-esteem and self-concept can also play a significant role in determining success and fulfillment. Individuals with a high self-esteem are more likely to pursue their goals, take risks, and challenge themselves, which can lead to personal growth and achievement. On the other hand, those with low self-esteem may hold themselves back, avoid opportunities, and limit their potential due to feelings of self-doubt and fear of failure. It is therefore essential for individuals to nurture and cultivate their self-esteem and self-concept in order to thrive and reach their full potential. These two constructs play a significant role in shaping how individuals view themselves, interact with others, and navigate the challenges of life. It is important for individuals to cultivate and maintain a positive self-esteem and self-concept in order to lead a fulfilling and successful life. By recognizing the influence of these factors on our thoughts, feelings, and behaviors, we can take steps to nurture our sense of self-worth and develop a more positive and balanced view of ourselves.

- Strategies for fostering a positive sense of identity

It encompasses various aspects, including one's race, ethnicity, gender, sexual orientation, and socioeconomic status, among others. A positive sense of identity is essential for overall well-being and mental health, as it influences how individuals perceive themselves and interact with the world around them. Fostering a positive sense of identity involves embracing diversity, promoting self-acceptance, and encouraging individuals to explore and celebrate their unique attributes. In this article, we will explore strategies for fostering a positive sense of identity, highlighting the importance of self-awareness, self-compassion, and self-affirmation in this process.

Embracing Diversity

One of the key strategies for fostering a positive sense of identity is embracing diversity. This involves recognizing and valuing the unique attributes and experiences of individuals from different backgrounds and cultures. Embracing diversity allows individuals to appreciate the richness of human differences and promotes a sense of inclusivity and belonging. When individuals are encouraged to embrace diversity, they are more likely to develop a more positive sense of identity, as they feel valued and respected for who they are.

Promoting Self-Acceptance

Another important strategy for fostering a positive sense of identity is promoting self-acceptance. This involves accepting and embracing all aspects of oneself, including one's strengths, weaknesses, quirks, and imperfections. Self-acceptance is crucial for developing a healthy self-image and building resilience in the face of challenges. By promoting self-acceptance, individuals can cultivate a sense of authenticity and self-worth that contributes to a positive sense of identity.

Encouraging Self-Exploration

Encouraging self-exploration is also essential for fostering a positive sense of identity. This involves providing individuals with opportunities to explore and reflect on their values, beliefs, interests, and goals. Through self-exploration, individuals can gain a deeper understanding of themselves and what truly matters to them. This process of self-discovery can lead to greater self-awareness and a more authentic sense of identity.

Celebrating Uniqueness

Celebrating uniqueness is another important strategy for fostering a positive sense of identity. This involves recognizing and celebrating the unique attributes and talents that make individuals who they are. By celebrating uniqueness, individuals can develop a strong sense of self-worth and confidence in their abilities. Celebrating uniqueness also fosters a culture of appreciation and acceptance, where differences are celebrated rather than stigmatized.

Cultivating Self-Compassion

Self-compassion is a critical aspect of fostering a positive sense of identity. This involves showing kindness and understanding towards oneself, especially in times of difficulty or failure. Self-compassion allows individuals to be more forgiving of their mistakes and shortcomings, leading to greater self-acceptance and resilience. By cultivating self-compassion, individuals can develop a more positive and nurturing relationship with themselves, which is essential for building a healthy sense of identity.

Practicing Self-Affirmation

Practicing self-affirmation is another effective strategy for fostering a positive sense of identity. This involves engaging in positive self-talk and affirming one's worth and abilities. By practicing self-affirmation, individuals can boost their self-esteem and confidence, leading to a more positive sense of identity. Self-affirmation can also help individuals overcome self-doubt and negative self-sabotaging beliefs, allowing them to embrace their true selves.

Conclusion

Fostering a positive sense of identity is crucial for overall well-being and mental health. By embracing diversity, promoting self-acceptance, encouraging self-exploration, celebrating uniqueness, cultivating self-compassion, and practicing self-affirmation, individuals can develop a strong and authentic sense of self. It is important for individuals to engage in self-reflection and self-care practices to nurture a positive sense of identity. By embracing and celebrating who they are, individuals can lead more fulfilling and authentic lives.

Chapter 6: Mental Health and Well-being in Adolescence

- COMMON MENTAL HEALTH challenges faced by teenagers

Teenagers today face a myriad of challenges when it comes to mental health. Adolescence is a time of great change, both physically and emotionally, as young people navigate the transition from childhood to adulthood. Many teenagers experience common mental health challenges that can have a profound impact on their well-being and overall quality of life. It is important for parents, educators, and healthcare professionals to be aware of these challenges and provide the necessary support and resources to help teenagers cope and thrive during this critical stage of development.

One of the most common mental health challenges faced by teenagers is anxiety. Anxiety disorders, such as generalized anxiety disorder, social anxiety disorder, and panic disorder, are prevalent among adolescents and can manifest in a variety of ways. Teenagers may experience persistent worry, fear, or irrational thoughts that interfere with their daily activities and relationships. Anxiety can also manifest physically, leading to symptoms such as restlessness, fatigue, and difficulty concentrating. It is important for parents and caregivers to recognize the signs of anxiety in teenagers and seek professional help if needed.

Depression is another common mental health challenge that affects many teenagers. Adolescents may experience feelings of sadness, hopelessness, and low self-esteem that persist for weeks or even months. Symptoms of depression can include changes in sleep and appetite, loss of interest in activities once enjoyed, and thoughts of suicide. It is crucial for parents and educators to pay attention to these warning signs and seek help from a mental health professional if a teenager is struggling with depression. Early intervention and support are essential in helping teenagers overcome this challenging mental health issue.

Substance abuse is also a major mental health challenge that many teenagers face. Adolescents may turn to drugs or alcohol as a way to cope with emotional pain, stress, or peer pressure. Substance abuse can have serious consequences on a teenager's physical and mental health, as well as their academic and social life. It is important for parents and educators to educate teenagers about the risks of substance abuse and provide healthy outlets for managing stress and emotions. Seeking help from a counselor or support group can also be beneficial for teenagers struggling with substance abuse.

Another common mental health challenge faced by teenagers is eating disorders. Conditions such as anorexia nervosa, bulimia nervosa, and binge eating disorder are prevalent among adolescents, especially young women. Eating disorders can have serious implications on a teenager's physical health, as well as their emotional well-being and self-esteem. Parents and caregivers should be vigilant in monitoring a teenager's eating habits and body image and seek help from a healthcare professional if there are concerns about an eating disorder. Early intervention and treatment are crucial in helping teenagers recover from this challenging mental health issue.

Self-harm is another mental health challenge that is prevalent among teenagers. Adolescents may engage in self-harming behaviors, such as cutting or burning themselves, as a way to cope with emotional pain or trauma. Self-harm is a serious issue that requires immediate attention and intervention from a mental health professional. Parents and educators should be aware of the warning signs of self-harm, such as unexplained cuts or bruises, and provide a supportive and non-judgmental environment for teenagers to talk about their feelings and seek help. It is important to address the underlying issues contributing to self-harm and develop healthy coping strategies for managing emotional distress. It is important for parents, educators, and healthcare professionals to be aware of these challenges and provide the necessary support and resources to help teenagers cope and thrive during this critical stage of development. By recognizing the signs of anxiety, depression, substance abuse, eating disorders, and self-harm, and seeking appropriate help and treatment, we can help teenagers navigate through these challenges and emerge stronger and more resilient on the other side.

- The importance of seeking help for mental health issues

Mental health is a crucial aspect of overall well-being, yet it is often overlooked or stigmatized in society. Seeking help for mental health issues is a vital step in improving one's quality of life and overall functioning. It is important to recognize when you are struggling and to reach out for support from professionals who are trained to help. Mental health issues can take many forms, including anxiety disorders, depression, trauma, and substance abuse. Ignoring these issues can have serious consequences on physical health, relationships, work performance, and overall happiness.

One of the main reasons why seeking help for mental health issues is so important is that these issues can significantly impact one's quality of life. Mental health problems can manifest in a variety of ways, such as difficulty sleeping, feeling constantly overwhelmed, or experiencing mood swings. These symptoms can interfere with daily activities and relationships, making it difficult to maintain a fulfilling and balanced life. By seeking help from a mental health professional, individuals can learn coping strategies, develop healthier ways of thinking and behaving, and ultimately improve their overall well-being.

Another reason why seeking help for mental health issues is crucial is that these issues can worsen over time if left untreated. Mental health problems are not something that can simply be ignored or pushed aside. Ignoring these issues can lead to increased stress, isolation, and a decreased ability to function in daily life. In some cases, untreated mental health issues can lead to more serious problems, such as self-harm or substance abuse. By seeking help early on, individuals can prevent their mental health issues from escalating and can begin the journey towards healing and recovery.

Furthermore, seeking help for mental health issues is important because it can lead to a better understanding of oneself and one's emotions. Many individuals who struggle with mental health issues may not fully understand the root causes of their problems or how to effectively address them. By working with a mental health professional, individuals can gain insight into their thought patterns, emotions, and behaviors, and can learn how to make positive changes in their lives. This self-awareness can be empowering and can lead to greater self-acceptance and self-esteem.

Additionally, seeking help for mental health issues can improve one's relationships with others. Mental health problems can often strain relationships with friends, family members, and romantic partners. Individuals who are struggling with mental health issues may find it difficult to communicate their needs, may withdraw from social activities, or may become irritable and argumentative. By seeking help for mental health issues, individuals can learn how to effectively communicate their feelings and needs to others, can improve their ability to empathize and connect with others, and can strengthen their interpersonal skills.

Another important reason to seek help for mental health issues is that mental health professionals are trained to provide evidence-based treatments and support. Mental health professionals, such as therapists, counselors, and psychiatrists, have the knowledge and skills to assess mental health issues, develop personalized treatment plans, and provide ongoing support and guidance. These professionals can offer a variety of therapeutic approaches, such as cognitive-behavioral therapy, medication management, and group therapy, that have been proven to be effective in treating mental health issues. By seeking help from a mental health professional, individuals can receive the care and support they need to overcome their mental health challenges. Mental health problems can have serious consequences on physical health, relationships, work performance, and overall happiness. By seeking help from a mental health professional, individuals can learn coping strategies, gain self-awareness, improve their relationships with others, and receive evidence-based treatments and support. It is important to recognize when you are struggling and to reach out for help, as doing so can lead to healing, growth, and a more fulfilling life.

- Strategies for maintaining overall well-being

Maintaining overall well-being is essential for a fulfilling and healthy life. It encompasses a holistic approach that addresses physical, mental, emotional, and social aspects of an individual's life. There are various strategies that can be implemented to achieve and sustain overall well-being, and it is important to tailor these strategies to fit one's unique needs and preferences. In this discussion, we will explore some key strategies for maintaining overall well-being and how they can be integrated into daily life for long-term success.

First and foremost, a balanced diet and regular exercise are foundational pillars of maintaining overall well-being. Eating a variety of nutrient-rich foods such as fruits, vegetables, whole grains, lean proteins, and healthy fats is crucial for maintaining optimal physical health. It is also important to stay hydrated by drinking plenty of water throughout the day. Regular exercise, whether it be cardio, strength training, yoga, or any other form of physical activity, not only improves physical health but also has numerous mental and emotional benefits. Exercise releases endorphins, which are known as the "feel-good" hormones, and can help reduce stress, anxiety, and symptoms of depression.

In addition to a healthy diet and regular exercise, getting an adequate amount of sleep is essential for overall well-being. Quality sleep is crucial for physical and mental restoration, immunity, and cognitive function. Adults should aim for 7-9 hours of quality sleep each night to ensure optimal health and well-being. Establishing a consistent sleep schedule, creating a relaxing bedtime routine, and optimizing your sleep environment can help improve the quality of your sleep and promote overall well-being.

Managing stress is another important aspect of maintaining overall well-being. Chronic stress can have detrimental effects on both physical and mental health, making it essential to develop effective stress management strategies. Some effective stress management techniques include deep breathing exercises, meditation, yoga, mindfulness practices, relaxation techniques, and engaging in activities that bring joy and relaxation. It is important to find what works best for you and incorporate stress-relief practices into your daily routine to promote overall well-being.

Building and maintaining positive relationships is also key to overall well-being. Strong social connections have been linked to improved mental health, longevity, and overall well-being. It is important to cultivate healthy relationships with friends, family, colleagues, and community members. Spending quality time with loved ones, engaging in meaningful conversations, and participating in social activities can all contribute to a sense of connection, belonging, and well-being. It is important to prioritize relationships and nurture them through open communication, empathy, and mutual support.

Another important aspect of maintaining overall well-being is taking care of your mental and emotional health. This includes practicing self-care, developing healthy coping mechanisms, and seeking help when needed. Self-care activities such as reading, journaling, taking a bath, going for a walk, or practicing a hobby can help reduce stress, improve mood, and promote overall well-being. Developing healthy coping mechanisms, such as setting boundaries, expressing emotions, and practicing self-compassion, can help you navigate life's challenges with resilience and grace. It is also important to seek professional help if you are struggling with mental health issues or emotional distress. By prioritizing healthy habits such as a balanced diet, regular exercise, quality sleep, stress management, positive relationships, and mental and emotional self-care, individuals can cultivate a strong foundation for optimal health and well-being. It is important to remember that well-being is a dynamic and ongoing process that requires self-awareness, commitment, and a willingness to adapt and grow. By integrating these strategies into your daily life and making them a priority, you can nurture your well-being and live a fulfilling and vibrant life.

Chapter 7: Communication Skills for Parents and Teens

- EFFECTIVE COMMUNICATION techniques for navigating conflicts

Conflict is an inevitable part of human interaction, and how we navigate it can greatly impact the quality of our relationships and the outcomes we achieve. Effective communication is essential in resolving conflicts, as it allows individuals to express their needs and concerns while also listening to and understanding the perspectives of others. In this essay, we will explore various communication techniques that can help individuals navigate conflicts successfully.

One important communication technique for navigating conflicts is active listening. Active listening involves fully focusing on what the other person is saying, without interrupting or formulating a response in your mind. By actively listening, you show the other person that you respect their perspective and are genuinely interested in understanding their point of view. This can help de-escalate conflicts and create a more productive and respectful dialogue.

Another key communication technique for navigating conflicts is using "I" statements. "I" statements focus on expressing your own thoughts, feelings, and needs, rather than placing blame or making assumptions about the other person. For example, instead of saying "You never listen to me," you could say "I feel frustrated when I don't feel heard. " Using "I" statements can help prevent defensiveness and promote open communication and understanding.

Nonverbal communication also plays a crucial role in navigating conflicts. Nonverbal cues such as facial expressions, body language, and tone of voice can communicate a lot about our emotions and intentions. For example, maintaining eye contact, using an open posture, and speaking calmly can help convey a sense of respect and cooperation during a conflict. Being mindful of your nonverbal communication can help ensure that your message is received clearly and that the other person feels heard and understood.

Effective communication techniques for navigating conflicts also include being assertive and setting boundaries. Being assertive means expressing your needs and concerns in a clear and confident manner, while also respecting the rights and boundaries of others. Setting boundaries can help prevent conflicts from escalating by establishing clear expectations and limits. For example, if someone is speaking to you in a disrespectful manner, you can assertively communicate that you will not tolerate such behavior and request that they communicate with you in a more respectful way.

Conflict resolution strategies such as compromise and collaboration can also be effective communication techniques for navigating conflicts. Compromise involves finding a middle ground that meets the needs of all parties involved, while collaboration involves working together to find a solution that satisfies everyone's interests. By adopting a problem-solving mindset and being open to considering different perspectives, individuals can overcome differences and reach mutually beneficial resolutions. By actively listening, using "I" statements, being mindful of nonverbal cues, being assertive, setting boundaries, and using conflict resolution strategies such as compromise and collaboration, individuals can promote understanding, respect, and cooperation in resolving conflicts. By incorporating these communication techniques into their interactions, individuals can build stronger and more positive relationships, both personally and professionally.

- The importance of active listening in parent-teen relationships

Active listening is a vital component of effective communication, particularly in parent-teen relationships. This process involves fully engaging with the speaker, demonstrating empathy, and providing feedback to ensure understanding. In the context of parent-teen relationships, active listening plays a crucial role in fostering mutual respect, trust, and understanding between family members. By actively listening to their teenagers, parents can establish open lines of communication, strengthen their bond, and create a supportive environment for their children to express themselves.

One of the primary reasons why active listening is important in parent-teen relationships is its role in establishing trust and respect. Adolescence is a critical period of development where teenagers are forming their identities, exploring new ideas, and asserting their independence. By actively listening to their teenagers, parents show that they value their opinions, thoughts, and feelings, which helps build trust and respect between family members. This, in turn, creates a strong foundation for healthy communication and fosters a sense of understanding and mutual support within the family.

Another significant benefit of active listening in parent-teen relationships is its role in promoting effective communication. Effective communication is essential for resolving conflicts, addressing issues, and navigating the challenges that arise during the teenage years. By actively listening to their teenagers, parents can better understand their perspective, emotions, and concerns, which enables them to respond in a thoughtful and empathetic manner. This type of communication fosters a positive and supportive environment where teenagers feel heard, validated, and respected, leading to healthier and more fulfilling relationships between parents and their children.

Furthermore, active listening also helps parents and teenagers build emotional intelligence and empathy. When parents actively listen to their teenagers, they not only show that they care about their children's well-being but also demonstrate empathy and understanding towards their experiences and emotions. By practicing active listening, parents can teach their teenagers valuable communication skills, such as emotional regulation, empathy, and perspective-taking, which are essential for healthy relationships and personal growth. This process allows parents and teenagers to better connect with one another on an emotional level, leading to deeper and more meaningful relationships within the family.

In addition to fostering trust, effective communication, and emotional intelligence, active listening also helps parents and teenagers navigate conflicts and challenges in a constructive and positive manner. Conflict is a natural part of any relationship, particularly between parents and teenagers who may have different perspectives, values, and priorities. By actively listening to their teenagers during conflicts, parents demonstrate respect, empathy, and understanding, which can de-escalate tensions and create a safe space for open and honest communication. This approach allows parents and teenagers to work through disagreements, find common ground, and develop effective strategies for resolving conflicts in a respectful and collaborative way.

Moreover, active listening in parent-teen relationships has been shown to improve teens' mental health and well-being. Adolescence is a period of heightened emotional intensity, stress, and vulnerability, where teenagers may experience a range of emotions, including anxiety, depression, and loneliness. By actively listening to their teenagers, parents can provide emotional support, validation, and understanding, which can help alleviate feelings of isolation, insecurity, and distress. This process also enables parents to identify potential signs of mental health issues, such as withdrawal, changes in behavior, or mood swings, and seek appropriate support and resources for their teenagers as needed. By actively listening to their teenagers, parents can establish trust, respect, and understanding, create a supportive environment for open communication, and promote healthy relationships within the family. This process also helps parents and teenagers develop emotional intelligence, empathy, and conflict resolution skills, which are essential for navigating the challenges of adolescence and fostering positive mental health and well-being. By practicing active listening, parents can strengthen their bond with their teenagers, enhance their communication skills, and build a strong and resilient family dynamic based on trust, respect, and mutual support.

- Building trust and openness in family communication

Effective family communication is a vital component of building trust and openness within the family unit. When family members communicate openly and honestly with one another, they are able to establish strong and meaningful relationships, as well as create a safe and supportive environment for sharing thoughts, feelings, and concerns. Trust is the foundation of any healthy relationship, and in a familial context, it is essential for fostering a sense of security, understanding, and connection among family members. By cultivating trust and openness in family communication, individuals can strengthen their bonds with one another, resolve conflicts more effectively, and ultimately create a harmonious family dynamic.

One of the key strategies for building trust and openness in family communication is active listening. Active listening involves not only hearing what is being said but also understanding and empathizing with the speaker's perspective. By truly listening to one another, family members can demonstrate respect, validation, and compassion, which in turn fosters trust and openness in communication. When family members feel heard and understood, they are more likely to feel comfortable expressing themselves honestly and authentically, which is essential for building a strong foundation of trust within the family.

Another important aspect of building trust and openness in family communication is promoting transparency and honesty. Open and honest communication is essential for creating a supportive and nurturing environment where family members can express their thoughts, feelings, and concerns without fear of judgment or retribution. By being transparent and honest with one another, family members can cultivate a sense of trust and mutual respect that is essential for maintaining healthy and harmonious relationships. When family members are open and honest in their communication, they are able to address conflicts, resolve misunderstandings, and work together to find solutions to common challenges.

In addition to active listening and honesty, establishing clear and effective communication boundaries is also crucial for building trust and openness within the family. Establishing boundaries helps family members respect each other's privacy, personal space, and emotional needs, which in turn fosters a sense of trust and security within the family unit. By setting boundaries in communication, family members can create a supportive and respectful environment where everyone feels valued, heard, and understood. Clear communication boundaries also help prevent misunderstandings, conflicts, and hurtful interactions, which can undermine trust and openness within the family.

Furthermore, creating a culture of empathy and understanding within the family is essential for building trust and openness in communication. Empathy involves putting oneself in another's shoes, understanding their feelings, and responding with kindness and compassion. By cultivating empathy within the family, family members can support one another through challenging times, validate each other's experiences, and build strong emotional connections that foster trust and openness in communication. When family members show empathy and understanding towards one another, they are able to create a nurturing and supportive environment where everyone feels valued, cared for, and respected. By practicing these strategies, family members can create a safe and supportive environment where they can communicate openly, honestly, and authentically with one another. Trust and openness in family communication are essential for building strong and meaningful relationships, resolving conflicts more effectively, and creating a harmonious family dynamic. By prioritizing trust and openness in communication, families can strengthen their bonds with one another and create a supportive and nurturing environment where everyone feels heard, understood, and valued.

Chapter 8: Academic and Career Planning for Teenagers

- THE IMPORTANCE OF setting goals and planning for the future

Setting goals and planning for the future are essential aspects of leading a successful and fulfilling life. By establishing clear objectives and creating a roadmap to achieve them, individuals can significantly increase their chances of reaching their desired outcomes. Whether these goals are related to personal growth, career advancement, financial stability, or any other aspect of life, having a plan in place can provide motivation, direction, and a sense of purpose.

One of the key benefits of setting goals and planning for the future is that it allows individuals to prioritize their actions and focus their energy on what truly matters to them. Without clear goals, individuals may find themselves drifting aimlessly through life, unsure of what they want to achieve or how to get there. This lack of direction can lead to feelings of frustration, apathy, and a sense of stagnation. In contrast, having well-defined goals in place can help individuals to stay focused, motivated, and proactive in working towards their objectives.

Additionally, setting goals and planning for the future can help individuals to overcome obstacles and challenges more effectively. By breaking down their long-term goals into smaller, manageable tasks, individuals can identify the steps they need to take to achieve their objectives. This systematic approach can help individuals to anticipate potential roadblocks, develop contingency plans, and stay adaptable in the face of unexpected setbacks. As a result, individuals are better equipped to navigate challenges and maintain their momentum towards their goals.

Furthermore, setting goals and planning for the future can empower individuals to take control of their lives and shape their own destinies. Instead of passively waiting for opportunities to come their way, individuals who have clear goals and a well-defined plan can proactively seek out the resources, knowledge, and support they need to turn their aspirations into reality. By taking ownership of their future and actively working towards their goals, individuals can cultivate a sense of agency, self-efficacy, and resilience that can positively impact all areas of their lives.

In addition to providing a sense of purpose and direction, setting goals and planning for the future can also help individuals to measure their progress and celebrate their achievements along the way. By breaking down their long-term goals into smaller milestones and tracking their progress towards these objectives, individuals can stay motivated and engaged in the pursuit of their aspirations. This sense of accomplishment can serve as a powerful source of motivation, reinforcing individuals' belief in their abilities and inspiring them to continue striving towards their goals. By establishing clear objectives, creating a roadmap to achieve them, and staying committed to their goals, individuals can enhance their focus, motivation, and resilience in the face of challenges. With a well-defined plan in place, individuals can take control of their lives, shape their own destinies, and work towards creating the future they desire. In doing so, individuals can unlock their full potential, achieve their aspirations, and lead a more purposeful and fulfilling life.

- Strategies for academic success and career exploration

Academic success and career exploration are two key components of a student's educational journey. To excel in both areas, students must develop effective strategies that will help them navigate the complexities of higher education and the job market. In this essay, we will discuss some practical and proven strategies that can help students achieve academic success and explore various career opportunities.

First and foremost, it is essential for students to set clear academic goals and develop a plan to achieve them. This includes identifying their strengths and areas for improvement, as well as understanding the requirements of their program of study. By setting specific, measurable, achievable, relevant, and time-bound (SMART) goals, students can stay motivated and focused on their academic pursuits. Additionally, creating a study schedule and utilizing time management techniques can help students stay organized and on track with their coursework.

Another important strategy for academic success is to actively engage in the learning process. This includes attending classes regularly, participating in discussions, asking questions, and seeking help when needed. By actively engaging with course material and interacting with professors and peers, students can deepen their understanding of the subject matter and improve their academic performance. Additionally, forming study groups and seeking out tutoring services can provide additional support and enhance the learning experience.

In addition to academic success, it is crucial for students to explore various career options and develop a plan for their future professional endeavors. Career exploration involves researching different industries, job roles, and companies, as well as gaining practical experience through internships, co-op programs, and volunteer opportunities. By exploring different career paths and gaining exposure to various fields, students can better understand their interests, values, and skills, and make informed decisions about their future career goals.

Networking is another important strategy for career exploration and success. Building professional relationships with professors, alumni, industry professionals, and peers can provide valuable insights, advice, and opportunities for career advancement. Attending career fairs, workshops, and networking events can also help students expand their professional network and learn more about job opportunities in their desired field. Additionally, creating a LinkedIn profile and maintaining an online presence can help students showcase their skills and accomplishments to potential employers.

In short, continuous learning and professional development are essential for academic success and career exploration. As technology and industries evolve, it is important for students to stay current with trends and developments in their field of study. This may involve attending conferences, workshops, and seminars, taking online courses, obtaining certifications, and pursuing further education. By continuously learning and expanding their knowledge and skills, students can improve their competitiveness in the job market and increase their chances of achieving long-term career success. By developing effective strategies such as setting clear goals, actively engaging in learning, exploring various career options, networking, and continuous learning and professional development, students can maximize their academic potential and pursue fulfilling career opportunities. With dedication, hard work, and a proactive approach, students can achieve their academic and career goals and pave the way for a successful and rewarding future.

- Balancing academic responsibilities with personal interests

Balancing academic responsibilities with personal interests can be a challenging task for many students, but it is essential for maintaining a healthy and well-rounded lifestyle. Academic responsibilities, such as attending classes, completing assignments, and studying for exams, are crucial for achieving success in school. However, personal interests, such as hobbies, sports, and social activities, are also important for personal growth and overall well-being.

One key strategy for balancing academic responsibilities with personal interests is effective time management. Students can create a schedule that allocates specific time blocks for studying, attending classes, and completing assignments, as well as time for pursuing personal interests. By prioritizing and organizing tasks effectively, students can ensure that they have enough time to devote to both their academic responsibilities and personal interests.

Another important aspect of balancing academic responsibilities with personal interests is setting realistic goals and expectations. It is essential for students to establish achievable goals for their academic work, while also recognizing the importance of taking breaks and pursuing activities that bring them joy and relaxation. By setting realistic goals and expectations, students can avoid feeling overwhelmed and maintain a healthy balance between their academic responsibilities and personal interests.

Additionally, having a supportive network of friends, family, and peers can help students in balancing their academic responsibilities with personal interests. Seeking help and guidance from others can provide students with valuable insight and advice on how to manage their time effectively, prioritize tasks, and achieve a healthy work-life balance. By surrounding themselves with a supportive community, students can feel empowered to pursue their personal interests while also excelling in their academic pursuits.

Furthermore, practicing self-care and prioritizing mental and physical well-being is crucial in balancing academic responsibilities with personal interests. Taking care of oneself, both physically and mentally, is essential for maintaining a strong work-life balance and avoiding burnout. Engaging in activities that promote relaxation, such as meditation, yoga, or spending time outdoors, can help students recharge and refocus their energy on their academic responsibilities and personal interests. By practicing effective time management, setting realistic goals and expectations, seeking support from others, and prioritizing self-care, students can achieve a healthy work-life balance and excel in both their academic pursuits and personal interests. Remember, it is important to prioritize both academic responsibilities and personal interests to maintain overall well-being and success in school and beyond.

Chapter 9: Navigating Technology and Social Media

- THE IMPACT OF TECHNOLOGY on teenage behavior and mental health

With the prevalence of smartphones, social media platforms, and online gaming, teenagers are constantly connected to a digital world that offers both opportunities and challenges. This paper explores the impact of technology on teenage behavior and mental health, examining the potential benefits and risks associated with their use of digital devices. By understanding how technology influences teenagers, we can better support their well-being and development in an increasingly digital age.

The Benefits of Technology for Teenagers

Technology offers a wide range of benefits for teenagers, providing them with access to information, resources, and opportunities that were previously unavailable. For example, smartphones and tablets allow teenagers to stay connected with friends and family, access educational materials, and pursue their interests through apps and online platforms. Social media platforms such as Instagram, Snapchat, and TikTok enable teenagers to share their experiences, connect with peers, and express themselves creatively. Online gaming platforms like Fortnite and Minecraft provide opportunities for teenagers to collaborate, compete, and problem-solve in virtual environments.

In addition, technology can enhance teenagers' learning experiences by providing access to educational resources, virtual classrooms, and interactive tools. For example, online learning platforms like Khan Academy and Coursera offer teenagers the opportunity to supplement their traditional education with personalized learning experiences. Virtual reality (VR) technology can also be used to create immersive learning environments that engage teenagers in interactive and hands-on experiences.

The Risks of Technology for Teenagers

While technology offers many benefits for teenagers, it also poses risks to their behavior and mental health. One of the primary concerns is the impact of excessive screen time on teenagers' physical and mental well-being. Research has shown that excessive screen time can lead to a sedentary lifestyle, poor sleep quality, and increased risk of obesity and other health problems. In addition, prolonged use of digital devices can contribute to eye strain, headaches, and musculoskeletal problems in teenagers.

Furthermore, technology can have a negative impact on teenagers' mental health by exacerbating feelings of loneliness, anxiety, and depression. Social media platforms, in particular, have been linked to increased rates of cyberbullying, social comparison, and low self-esteem among teenagers. The pressure to present a curated and idealized version of oneself online can lead to feelings of inadequacy and insecurity. Moreover, the constant exposure to online content, such as violent or graphic images, can desensitize teenagers to real-world violence and trauma.

Another concern is the potential for addiction to technology among teenagers, especially to online gaming, social media, and other digital platforms. Research has shown that excessive use of digital devices can trigger addictive behaviors, leading to withdrawal symptoms, loss of interest in other activities, and difficulty controlling one's impulses. Therefore, it is important to recognize the potential risks of technology and establish healthy technology habits for teenagers to promote their well-being and mental health.

Strategies for Supporting Teenagers' Well-being in a Digital Age

To support teenagers' well-being in a digital age, it is essential to implement strategies that promote healthy technology use and address the potential risks associated with digital devices. One approach is to establish clear boundaries and limits around screen time, encouraging teenagers to balance their use of technology with offline activities such as exercise, hobbies, and socializing with friends. Parents can set rules and guidelines for device use, such as designated times for screen-free activities, tech-free zones in the home, and restrictions on accessing digital devices before bedtime.

Moreover, it is important to educate teenagers about the potential risks of technology, such as cyberbullying, online harassment, and exposure to inappropriate content. By fostering open and honest conversations about online safety and digital citizenship, teenagers can develop the skills and knowledge needed to navigate the digital world responsibly. Schools can also play a role in promoting digital literacy and cyber safety through initiatives such as digital citizenship programs, online safety workshops, and media literacy curriculum.

Furthermore, it is important to promote positive and healthy online behavior among teenagers by cultivating a supportive and inclusive online community. Educators, parents, and teenagers themselves can work together to create a culture of respect, empathy, and kindness in online interactions. By modeling positive online behavior and standing up against cyberbullying and harassment, teenagers can contribute to a more positive and safe online environment for themselves and their peers. While technology provides teenagers with access to information, resources, and opportunities that support their personal growth and development, it also poses risks such as excessive screen time, cyberbullying, and addiction. By implementing strategies that promote healthy technology use, educate teenagers about online safety, and foster positive online behaviors, we can support teenagers in navigating the digital world responsibly and promoting their well-being in a digital age. It is essential for parents, educators, and teenagers themselves to work together to create a culture of digital literacy, online safety, and positive online interactions that empower teenagers to make informed and responsible choices in their use of technology.

- Setting boundaries and limits around technology use

In today's digital age, the use of technology plays a significant role in our daily lives. With the increasing presence of smartphones, tablets, and laptops, it has become more challenging to disconnect from technology and establish boundaries around its use. Setting limits on technology use is crucial for maintaining a healthy balance between the virtual world and the real world. It is essential for individuals to be mindful of their technology usage and to create boundaries that allow for uninterrupted moments of rest and relaxation.

One of the primary reasons why setting boundaries around technology use is important is because excessive screen time can have detrimental effects on our mental and physical well-being. Research has shown that prolonged exposure to screens can lead to eye strain, disrupted sleep patterns, and increased feelings of anxiety and stress. By setting limits on technology use, individuals can reduce their risk of experiencing these negative effects and create a healthier relationship with technology.

Furthermore, excessive use of technology can lead to a decrease in productivity and concentration. The constant notifications and distractions from our devices can make it challenging to focus on tasks and complete them efficiently. By establishing boundaries around technology use, individuals can create dedicated periods of time for work or study without the interference of digital distractions. This can lead to increased productivity, better time management, and improved overall performance in various aspects of life.

In addition to the negative impact on our mental and physical well-being, excessive technology use can also have detrimental effects on our relationships. Spending too much time on our devices can lead to decreased face-to-face interactions with loved ones, which can weaken the quality of our relationships. By setting boundaries around technology use, individuals can prioritize spending quality time with friends and family without the distractions of screens. This can help strengthen relationships, improve communication, and foster deeper connections with those we care about.

When it comes to setting boundaries around technology use, it is important to be intentional and mindful of our habits. One way to establish boundaries is to create designated tech-free zones in the home, such as the dinner table or the bedroom. By establishing these areas as technology-free zones, individuals can create opportunities for meaningful interactions and moments of relaxation without the interference of screens. It is also helpful to set specific times during the day when technology use is allowed, such as during work hours or after completing essential tasks.

Another effective way to set boundaries around technology use is to practice digital detoxes or screen-free days. Taking a break from technology periodically can help individuals reset their minds, reduce feelings of stress and overwhelm, and reconnect with the world around them. By incorporating digital detoxes into their routine, individuals can develop a healthier relationship with technology and regain a sense of balance in their lives.

It is essential for individuals to prioritize self-care and well-being by setting boundaries around their technology use. By being intentional about how and when we engage with technology, we can create a healthy balance between the virtual world and the real world. Setting limits on technology use can help improve our mental and physical health, increase productivity, strengthen relationships, and promote overall well-being. By taking proactive steps to establish boundaries around technology use, we can create a more mindful and fulfilling relationship with technology in our daily lives.

- Promoting responsible digital citizenship

In today's digital age, promoting responsible digital citizenship is more important than ever before. With the proliferation of social media, online forums, and digital platforms, individuals have unprecedented access to information and the ability to connect with people from all corners of the globe. While this connectivity can bring about many positive outcomes, such as fostering cross-cultural understanding and facilitating communication, it also raises concerns about privacy, cyberbullying, misinformation, and online harassment. Therefore, it is essential for individuals to understand the importance of being responsible digital citizens and to actively engage in practices that promote safety, respect, and ethical behavior in the digital sphere.

One of the key aspects of promoting responsible digital citizenship is educating individuals about the potential risks and consequences of their online actions. Many people may not realize the impact that their digital footprint can have on their reputation, future opportunities, and even their safety. For example, posting compromising or inappropriate content online can not only harm an individual's reputation but also make them vulnerable to cyberbullying and online harassment. By raising awareness about these risks and encouraging individuals to think critically about their online behavior, we can help cultivate a culture of digital responsibility.

Another important aspect of promoting responsible digital citizenship is fostering a culture of respect and empathy online. In the digital world, it can be easy for individuals to hide behind the anonymity of a screen and engage in behavior that they would never consider in face-to-face interactions. This can lead to instances of cyberbullying, harassment, and hate speech, which can have serious consequences for individuals' mental health and well-being. By encouraging individuals to treat others with kindness, respect, and empathy online, we can create a more inclusive and positive digital environment where everyone feels safe and valued.

Furthermore, promoting responsible digital citizenship also involves teaching individuals about the importance of critical thinking and media literacy in the digital age. With the abundance of information available online, it can be challenging to discern fact from fiction and navigate the complex landscape of misinformation and disinformation. By equipping individuals with the skills to evaluate sources, analyze information critically, and verify the accuracy of content, we can empower them to make informed decisions and resist the spread of fake news and conspiracy theories. This not only benefits individuals in their personal lives but also contributes to a more informed and democratic society as a whole.

Additionally, promoting responsible digital citizenship entails advocating for policies and practices that protect individuals' privacy and data security online. In an increasingly digitalized world, personal information is constantly being collected, stored, and shared by companies, governments, and other entities. This raises concerns about data breaches, identity theft, and unauthorized surveillance, which can have serious repercussions for individuals' privacy and autonomy. By promoting transparency, accountability, and data protection measures, we can ensure that individuals have greater control over their personal information and are able to use digital platforms safely and securely. By raising awareness about the importance of ethical behavior, respect, critical thinking, and privacy online, we can empower individuals to navigate the digital landscape responsibly and contribute to a more inclusive, safe, and democratic digital society. It is crucial for us to recognize the opportunities and challenges that come with living in a digital age and actively engage in practices that promote responsible digital citizenship for the benefit of all.

Chapter 10: Resilience and Coping Strategies for Adolescents

- BUILDING RESILIENCE in the face of challenges

Resilience, the ability to bounce back from setbacks and adversity, is a crucial trait to cultivate in order to navigate life's challenges with grace and strength. Building resilience in the face of challenges requires a combination of self-awareness, emotional regulation, cognitive flexibility, and social support. By developing these skills and strategies, individuals can better cope with stress, adversity, and setbacks, and ultimately thrive in the face of life's inevitable obstacles.

One key aspect of building resilience is developing self-awareness. This involves recognizing one's thoughts, emotions, and behaviors, and understanding how they impact one's ability to cope with challenges. By being aware of our internal state, we can identify when we are feeling overwhelmed, stressed, or discouraged, and take proactive steps to address these emotions before they escalate. This could involve engaging in self-care activities, such as meditation, exercise, or spending time with loved ones, to recharge and refocus our energy in a positive direction.

Emotional regulation is another important skill in building resilience. This involves the ability to manage and control one's emotions in a healthy and constructive way. When faced with challenges, it is natural to experience a range of emotions, from fear and frustration to sadness and anger. By learning to regulate our emotions, we can prevent ourselves from becoming overwhelmed or reacting impulsively in difficult situations. This could involve practicing mindfulness techniques, such as deep breathing or progressive muscle relaxation, to calm the mind and body in times of stress.

Cognitive flexibility is also essential in building resilience. This involves the ability to adapt to new information and perspectives, and to see challenges as opportunities for growth and learning. When faced with obstacles, individuals with cognitive flexibility are able to reframe negative thoughts and beliefs, and see setbacks as temporary and surmountable. This mindset empowers individuals to find creative solutions to problems, and to persevere in the face of adversity. By fostering a growth mindset and challenging negative thought patterns, individuals can build resilience and thrive in the face of challenges.

Social support is another key component of building resilience. Humans are social creatures, and having a strong support network of friends, family, and mentors is crucial for navigating life's challenges. When faced with adversity, seeking support from others can provide emotional validation, practical advice, and a sense of belonging and connection. By surrounding ourselves with positive and supportive individuals who lift us up and encourage us to persevere, we can build resilience and weather life's storms with grace and strength. By cultivating these skills and strategies, individuals can better navigate life's obstacles and setbacks, and thrive in the face of adversity. By recognizing and managing our emotions, reframing negative thought patterns, and seeking support from others, we can build resilience and face life's challenges with grace and strength. Ultimately, resilience is a skill that can be learned and cultivated, and with practice and dedication, individuals can build the resilience needed to thrive in the face of life's inevitable challenges.

- Coping strategies for managing stress and anxiety

In today's fast-paced and demanding world, stress and anxiety have become increasingly common experiences for many individuals. Whether it's due to work pressures, financial concerns, relationship issues, or any number of other factors, the impact of stress and anxiety on our mental and physical well-being cannot be overstated. Fortunately, there are coping strategies that can help us manage and even reduce the negative effects of these overwhelming emotions.

One of the most effective coping strategies for managing stress and anxiety is developing a healthy lifestyle. This includes eating a balanced diet, getting regular exercise, and ensuring an adequate amount of sleep each night. Studies have shown that a healthy lifestyle can help improve mood, reduce stress levels, and increase overall feelings of well-being. Additionally, activities such as yoga, meditation, and deep breathing exercises can be beneficial in alleviating stress and anxiety. These practices can help calm the mind and promote a sense of relaxation and inner peace.

Another important coping strategy for managing stress and anxiety is practicing mindfulness. Mindfulness involves focusing on the present moment and accepting it without judgment. By being mindful, individuals can learn to detach themselves from negative thoughts and emotions, allowing them to experience greater clarity and calmness. Mindfulness techniques can include meditation, body scanning, and mindful breathing exercises. Research has shown that mindfulness can significantly reduce stress and anxiety, as well as improve overall mental health.

Additionally, building a strong support network can be essential in coping with stress and anxiety. Having friends, family members, or other trusted individuals to talk to and lean on during challenging times can provide immense comfort and reassurance. Social connections have been shown to help reduce feelings of loneliness, boost self-esteem, and increase feelings of security and belonging. It's important to reach out to others when feeling overwhelmed or anxious, as bottling up emotions can exacerbate stress and anxiety. Seeking professional help from a therapist or counselor can also be incredibly beneficial in learning coping strategies and developing healthier ways of managing stress and anxiety.

Furthermore, practicing self-care is a crucial aspect of coping with stress and anxiety. Taking time for oneself, engaging in activities that bring joy and relaxation, and prioritizing personal well-being are all essential components of self-care. This can include activities such as reading a book, taking a bath, going for a walk in nature, or listening to soothing music. By incorporating self-care practices into daily routines, individuals can better cope with stress and anxiety and cultivate a greater sense of balance and fulfillment in their lives. By implementing coping strategies such as developing a healthy lifestyle, practicing mindfulness, building a strong support network, and prioritizing self-care, individuals can effectively reduce the negative impact of these overwhelming emotions and improve their overall well-being. It's important to remember that everyone experiences stress and anxiety differently and that what works for one person may not work for another. It may take time and experimentation to find the coping strategies that are most effective for each individual. With persistence and determination, however, it is possible to overcome stress and anxiety and lead a happier, more balanced life.

- Seeking support and practicing self-care

Seeking support and practicing self-care are essential aspects of maintaining mental and emotional well-being. In today's fast-paced and often overwhelming world, it is important to recognize when we need help and to actively engage in activities that promote self-care. Whether it be seeking therapy, talking to a friend, or engaging in activities that help us relax and recharge, taking care of ourselves is crucial in order to navigate the challenges and stresses of daily life. This article aims to explore the importance of seeking support and practicing self-care, as well as provide practical tips and strategies for incorporating these practices into our daily routines.

One of the key reasons why seeking support and practicing self-care is important is because it helps us to better cope with the various stressors and challenges that life throws our way. By seeking support from a therapist, counselor, or support group, we can gain valuable insights, tools, and strategies for managing our emotions and navigating difficult situations. Additionally, talking to a friend or loved one can provide us with a sense of connection and validation, which can be incredibly comforting during times of distress. Engaging in self-care activities such as exercise, meditation, or spending time in nature, can help us relax, unwind, and recharge our batteries, which in turn can help us to better cope with stress and improve our overall well-being.

Furthermore, seeking support and practicing self-care can help us to build resilience and develop healthy coping mechanisms. By learning how to effectively manage our emotions and stress, we can develop the skills and confidence needed to face challenges head on and come out stronger on the other side. Engaging in self-care activities that nurture our mind, body, and spirit can help us to cultivate a sense of inner peace and balance, which can be incredibly empowering as we navigate the ups and downs of life. Additionally, the support and guidance we receive from others can help us to gain new perspectives, challenge negative beliefs, and learn how to better communicate our needs and boundaries.

It is important to remember that seeking support and practicing self-care is not a sign of weakness, but rather a proactive step towards prioritizing our mental and emotional well-being. In our society, there is often a stigma surrounding mental health and self-care, which can make it difficult for individuals to reach out for help or prioritize their own needs. However, it is important to remember that taking care of ourselves is not selfish or indulgent, but rather a necessary part of maintaining our overall health and well-being. By seeking support and engaging in activities that promote self-care, we can cultivate a sense of self-awareness, self-compassion, and self-empowerment that can help us to navigate life's challenges with grace and resilience. By reaching out for help when needed and engaging in activities that promote self-care, we can better cope with stress, build resilience, and cultivate a sense of inner peace and balance. It is important to remember that taking care of ourselves is not selfish or indulgent, but rather a necessary part of prioritizing our own needs and well-being. By incorporating support and self-care practices into our daily routines, we can better navigate life's challenges and lead happier, healthier, and more fulfilling lives.

Chapter 11: The Impact of Family Dynamics on Teenage Development

- THE ROLE OF FAMILY relationships in adolescent behavior

Adolescence is a period of significant growth and change, both physically and emotionally. During this time, adolescents are navigating the challenges of developing their identity, forming relationships, and establishing independence from their families. Family relationships play a crucial role in shaping adolescent behavior and development, as they provide the foundation for social and emotional growth. The dynamics within a family can have a profound impact on the way adolescents think, feel, and behave, influencing their choices and behaviors both in the present and in the future.

One of the key ways in which family relationships influence adolescent behavior is through the communication patterns within the family unit. Effective communication is essential for building trust and understanding between family members, and open and honest communication can help adolescents feel supported and valued. When families communicate effectively, adolescents are more likely to express their thoughts and feelings, seek guidance from their parents, and feel comfortable sharing their experiences. This can lead to healthier relationships and a greater sense of connectedness within the family, which in turn can positively impact adolescent behavior.

On the other hand, poor communication within the family can lead to misunderstandings, conflicts, and feelings of isolation among adolescents. When communication breaks down, adolescents may struggle to express themselves, feel unheard or misunderstood, and may resort to negative behaviors as a way of coping with their emotions. This can result in a cycle of conflict and tension within the family, further straining relationships and creating additional challenges for adolescents as they navigate the complexities of adolescence. Therefore, promoting effective communication within the family is essential for supporting positive adolescent behavior and development.

In addition to communication, the quality of the parent-child relationship also plays a significant role in shaping adolescent behavior. A warm and supportive parent-child relationship can foster a sense of security and trust in adolescents, providing them with the emotional support they need to navigate the challenges of adolescence. When parents are nurturing, responsive, and involved in their child's life, adolescents are more likely to develop positive self-esteem, resilience, and adaptive coping strategies. This can lead to healthier social relationships, better academic performance, and overall well-being in adolescents.

Conversely, harsh or inconsistent parenting practices can have a detrimental impact on adolescent behavior. Authoritarian parenting styles, for example, characterized by strict rules, punishment, and lack of warmth, can lead to feelings of resentment, rebellion, and low self-esteem in adolescents. Similarly, neglectful or permissive parenting styles can result in feelings of insecurity, lack of boundaries, and a lack of guidance in adolescents. These parenting behaviors can contribute to a range of negative outcomes, including delinquency, substance abuse, and mental health issues in adolescents. Therefore, promoting positive parent-child relationships based on warmth, support, and clear communication is essential for supporting healthy adolescent behavior.

Furthermore, the role of siblings and extended family members in shaping adolescent behavior should not be overlooked. Siblings can serve as important sources of support, companionship, and conflict resolution for adolescents, helping them develop social skills, empathy, and perspective-taking abilities. Positive sibling relationships can foster a sense of belonging and connectedness in adolescents, promoting emotional well-being and resilience. However, sibling conflict and rivalry can also have negative effects on adolescent behavior, leading to increased aggression, competition, and insecurity. Therefore, promoting healthy sibling relationships based on mutual respect, cooperation, and communication is important for supporting positive adolescent behavior.

Extended family members, such as grandparents, aunts, uncles, and cousins, can also play a significant role in shaping adolescent behavior. These relationships can provide adolescents with additional sources of support, guidance, and cultural identity, helping them navigate the complexities of adolescence with a sense of belonging and connectedness to their heritage and traditions. However, family dynamics within extended family relationships can vary widely, and conflicts or tensions within these relationships can impact adolescent behavior in both positive and negative ways. Therefore, fostering positive relationships with extended family members and promoting open communication and mutual respect can enhance adolescent well-being and development. The communication patterns within the family, the quality of the parent-child relationship, and the influence of siblings and extended family members all contribute to the way adolescents think, feel, and behave. By promoting positive family relationships based on warmth, support, and effective communication, parents and caregivers can help adolescents navigate the challenges of adolescence with resilience and confidence. A supportive family environment can foster emotional well-being, social connectedness, and positive behavioral outcomes in adolescents, setting the stage for healthy development and well-being in the long term.

- Common family dynamics that impact teenage well-being

Teenage well-being is a complex and multifaceted issue that is influenced by a wide range of factors, including family dynamics. The family unit plays a crucial role in shaping the emotional, social, and psychological development of adolescents, and the way in which family members interact with one another can have a significant impact on a teenager's overall well-being. In this essay, we will explore some of the common family dynamics that can either support or hinder the well-being of teenagers, and discuss strategies for fostering positive family relationships that promote the health and happiness of adolescents.

One of the most important family dynamics that can impact teenage well-being is the quality of the parent-child relationship. Research has consistently shown that adolescents who have strong, supportive relationships with their parents are more likely to have higher levels of self-esteem, better emotional regulation, and reduced risk of developing mental health issues such as depression and anxiety. Positive parent-child relationships are characterized by open communication, mutual respect, and emotional connection, and parents who are able to provide a safe and nurturing environment for their teenagers are more likely to raise emotionally healthy and well-adjusted children.

On the other hand, negative parent-child relationships can have a detrimental effect on teenage well-being. Conflictual or hostile interactions between parents and teenagers can lead to heightened levels of stress, anxiety, and depression in adolescents, and can also contribute to the development of behavioural problems such as substance abuse and delinquency. In families where communication is poor, boundaries are unclear, and conflict is frequent, teenagers may struggle to develop a sense of identity and purpose, which can impact their overall well-being and future success.

Another common family dynamic that can impact teenage well-being is the presence of sibling relationships. Siblings play a unique role in the lives of teenagers, as they are often the first and most enduring social connections that adolescents have outside of their parents. Positive sibling relationships can provide teenagers with emotional support, companionship, and opportunities for social learning and growth. Siblings who are able to communicate openly, resolve conflicts peacefully, and show empathy and understanding towards one another are more likely to have positive well-being outcomes.

However, sibling relationships can also be a source of stress and conflict for teenagers, particularly in families where there is a large age gap between siblings, or where sibling rivalry and competition are prevalent. Sibling conflict can lead to feelings of jealousy, resentment, and low self-esteem in teenagers, and can hinder their ability to form healthy social relationships outside of the family unit. Parents can play a key role in supporting positive sibling relationships by fostering a sense of cooperation and collaboration between siblings, and by modelling respectful and supportive behaviour in their own relationships with their children.

In addition to the parent-child and sibling dynamics, the overall family environment can also play a significant role in shaping teenage well-being. Families that are characterized by warmth, stability, and consistency are more likely to promote the emotional and social development of adolescents, while families that are marked by chaos, unpredictability, and conflict may hinder teenage well-being. Research has shown that teenagers who come from families where there is a strong sense of cohesion, shared values, and positive communication are more likely to have better mental health outcomes and higher levels of life satisfaction.

Conversely, families that lack cohesion, structure, and emotional support can contribute to feelings of loneliness, isolation, and insecurity in teenagers, which can impact their overall well-being and sense of self-worth. In families where there is a lack of emotional support or where teenagers feel disconnected from their family members, adolescents may be more vulnerable to developing mental health issues such as depression, anxiety, and substance abuse. It is important for parents to create a supportive and nurturing family environment that encourages open communication, emotional expression, and mutual respect in order to promote the well-being of their teenage children. Positive parent-child relationships, supportive sibling dynamics, and a nurturing family environment are all key factors that can contribute to the emotional, social, and psychological development of adolescents. By fostering open communication, emotional connection, and mutual respect within the family unit, parents can help to support the well-being of their teenage children and promote their overall health and happiness. By recognizing the impact that family dynamics can have on teenage well-being, parents and caregivers can work towards creating a supportive and nurturing family environment that fosters positive relationships and promotes the well-being of adolescents.

- Strategies for fostering positive family communication and relationships

Strong family communication and relationships are the cornerstone of a healthy and happy family dynamic. In order to foster positive communication and relationships within the family unit, it is important to establish clear communication channels, practice active listening, and prioritize quality time together. By implementing strategies that prioritize open and honest communication, families can build trust, strengthen their bond, and navigate conflicts more effectively.

One of the key strategies for fostering positive family communication is to establish clear communication channels within the family unit. This can be done by creating a safe space for open and honest dialogue, encouraging each family member to express their thoughts and feelings without fear of judgment or criticism. By setting aside time for regular family meetings or discussions, families can ensure that everyone has the opportunity to be heard and understood. Additionally, utilizing technology such as group chats or shared calendars can help keep everyone in the loop and facilitate communication between family members, especially in today's digital age.

Active listening is another critical component of positive family communication. This involves listening to what others are saying without interrupting, judging, or formulating a response in your head. By practicing active listening, family members can show empathy and understanding towards one another, which can strengthen their relationship and build trust. Encouraging family members to ask clarifying questions and repeat back what they have heard can also help ensure that everyone is on the same page and avoid misunderstandings.

Quality time spent together as a family is essential for building strong relationships and fostering positive communication. This can involve participating in activities that everyone enjoys, such as game nights, family dinners, or outdoor adventures. By creating opportunities for shared experiences and bonding, families can create lasting memories and deepen their connection with one another. Additionally, setting aside designated family time each week can help reinforce the importance of prioritizing your family relationships and ensure that everyone feels valued and supported.

In addition to these strategies, families can also benefit from developing conflict resolution skills to navigate disagreements and challenges effectively. By teaching family members how to communicate assertively, listen actively, and seek compromise, families can work through conflicts in a healthy and constructive manner. Encouraging family members to use "I" statements and express their feelings and needs clearly can help prevent misunderstandings and defuse tension. By approaching conflicts with an open mind and a willingness to find common ground, families can strengthen their relationships and learn to resolve disagreements more peacefully. By implementing these strategies and prioritizing the importance of family bonds, families can create a supportive and nurturing environment where everyone feels heard, understood, and valued. Through effective communication and strong relationships, families can build a foundation of trust and love that will withstand the test of time and help them navigate life's challenges together.

Chapter 12: Substance Use and Abuse in Adolescence

- THE RISKS AND CONSEQUENCES of substance use in teenagers

Substance use among teenagers is a growing concern in today's society, with potentially serious risks and consequences for their physical and mental health. It is essential to understand the potential dangers associated with substance use in teenagers in order to prevent and address any harmful behaviors. By examining the various substances commonly used by teenagers, such as alcohol, tobacco, marijuana, and prescription medications, we can gain a better understanding of the potential risks and consequences that teenagers may face.

Alcohol is one of the most commonly abused substances by teenagers, with significant consequences for their health and well-being. Teenagers who engage in heavy or binge drinking are at increased risk for a variety of negative outcomes, including impaired cognitive function, increased risk of accidents and injuries, and long-term health problems such as liver damage and addiction. Additionally, alcohol use among teenagers is associated with a higher likelihood of engaging in risky behaviors, such as unprotected sex and driving under the influence, which can have serious consequences for their safety and the safety of others.

Tobacco use is another prevalent issue among teenagers, with significant risks and consequences for their health. Smoking cigarettes or using other tobacco products can lead to a host of health problems, including respiratory issues, heart disease, and cancer. Teenagers who smoke are also more likely to develop a nicotine addiction, making it difficult for them to quit and increasing their risk of long-term health problems. Additionally, the social and financial costs of tobacco use can be significant for teenagers, impacting their relationships and future prospects.

Marijuana use is becoming increasingly common among teenagers, with potential risks and consequences that warrant attention. While many people view marijuana as a relatively harmless substance, especially compared to alcohol or tobacco, it can still have negative effects on teenagers' health and well-being. Teenagers who use marijuana may experience impaired cognitive function, memory and attention problems, and an increased risk of mental health issues such as depression and anxiety. Additionally, regular marijuana use during adolescence has been linked to lower academic achievement and an increased likelihood of dropping out of school.

Prescription medication misuse is a concerning trend among teenagers, with serious risks and consequences for their health. Many teenagers mistakenly believe that prescription medications are safer than illegal drugs, but the misuse of prescription drugs can be just as dangerous and addictive. Teenagers who abuse prescription medications, such as opioids, stimulants, or benzodiazepines, are at risk for a variety of negative outcomes, including overdose, addiction, and long-term health problems. Additionally, the misuse of prescription medications can have serious consequences for teenagers' relationships, academic performance, and future prospects. By understanding the various substances commonly used by teenagers and the potential dangers associated with them, parents, educators, and healthcare professionals can work together to prevent and address substance use in teenagers. It is important to educate teenagers about the risks and consequences of substance use, provide access to resources and support for those struggling with addiction, and create a supportive and nonjudgmental environment in which teenagers feel comfortable seeking help. By taking a proactive approach to addressing substance use among teenagers, we can help protect their health and well-being and set them on a path towards a healthier and brighter future.

- Signs of substance abuse and addiction

Substance abuse and addiction are complex issues that can have a profound impact on individuals and society as a whole. Understanding the signs and symptoms of substance abuse and addiction is crucial in order to provide appropriate support and intervention for those in need. This article will explore common signs of substance abuse and addiction, as well as potential risk factors and treatment options.

One of the most common signs of substance abuse and addiction is a persistent and compulsive use of a substance despite negative consequences. This can manifest as a strong desire or craving for the substance, an inability to control or limit use, and continued use even when faced with adverse effects on one's health, relationships, or finances. Individuals struggling with substance abuse and addiction may also experience withdrawal symptoms when attempting to cut back or stop using the substance, leading to a cycle of dependence and relapse.

Other signs of substance abuse and addiction may include changes in behavior, mood, or physical appearance. For example, individuals may become increasingly secretive or defensive about their substance use, engage in risky behaviors to obtain or use the substance, or exhibit sudden changes in mood or personality. Physical signs of substance abuse can range from weight loss or gain, to bloodshot eyes, slurred speech, or tremors. It is important to note that these signs may vary depending on the substance being used, as different substances can have different effects on the body and mind.

In addition to these outward signs, there are also underlying risk factors that may contribute to the development of substance abuse and addiction. These can include genetic predisposition, environmental influences, mental health disorders, trauma or stress, and a lack of healthy coping mechanisms. Individuals with a family history of substance abuse, a history of trauma or abuse, or co-occurring mental health disorders may be at a higher risk for developing substance abuse and addiction. It is important to consider these risk factors when assessing and addressing substance abuse issues in order to provide more personalized and effective treatment.

When it comes to addressing substance abuse and addiction, early intervention and access to treatment are key. There are a variety of treatment options available, including detoxification, residential treatment, outpatient programs, therapy, counseling, and support groups. Each individual may respond differently to treatment, so it is important to tailor interventions to meet their specific needs and circumstances. It is also important to take a holistic approach to treatment, addressing not only the physical aspects of substance abuse, but also the psychological, emotional, and social factors that may contribute to the problem. By recognizing the common signs and symptoms of substance abuse, as well as the underlying risk factors that may contribute to the problem, individuals and communities can take proactive steps to address this widespread issue. Through early intervention, personalized treatment, and ongoing support, individuals struggling with substance abuse and addiction can find the help they need to overcome these challenges and lead healthier, more fulfilling lives.

- Resources for prevention and intervention

Preventing and intervening in various issues such as mental health disorders, substance abuse, and domestic violence is essential for promoting individual and community well-being. There are a multitude of resources available to support prevention and intervention efforts, ranging from government agencies and nonprofit organizations to community-based programs and online resources. By utilizing these resources effectively, individuals and communities can work towards reducing the prevalence and impact of these issues and improving overall quality of life.

One key resource for prevention and intervention is government agencies, such as the Substance Abuse and Mental Health Services Administration (SAMHSA) and the Centers for Disease Control and Prevention (CDC). These agencies provide valuable information, funding, and support for programs aimed at preventing and addressing various health-related issues. For example, SAMHSA offers grants for substance abuse prevention and treatment programs, while the CDC provides data and resources on various public health issues, such as infectious diseases and mental health disorders. By leveraging the expertise and resources of government agencies, organizations and communities can develop more effective prevention and intervention strategies.

Nonprofit organizations are another important resource for prevention and intervention efforts. These organizations often specialize in specific issues, such as domestic violence or mental health, and provide a range of services, such as counseling, support groups, and advocacy. For example, the National Alliance on Mental Illness (NAMI) offers education and support to individuals and families affected by mental health disorders, while the National Coalition

Against Domestic Violence (NCADV) works to raise awareness and prevent domestic violence. By partnering with nonprofit organizations, communities can access specialized services and support tailored to their specific needs.

In addition to government agencies and nonprofit organizations, community-based programs play a crucial role in prevention and intervention efforts. These programs are often led by local stakeholders, such as schools, churches, and community centers, and focus on addressing issues within a specific community or population. For example, a school-based program may provide education on substance abuse prevention, while a church-based program may offer support services for victims of domestic violence. By engaging with and supporting community-based programs, individuals and organizations can work together to address issues at the grassroots level and create lasting change within their communities.

Online resources are also valuable tools for prevention and intervention. Websites and apps provide access to information, resources, and support services for individuals affected by various issues. For example, the National Institute on Drug Abuse (NIDA) offers online resources on substance abuse prevention and treatment, while the National Domestic Violence Hotline provides confidential support and resources for victims of domestic violence. By utilizing online resources, individuals can access information and support at any time, from anywhere, which can be especially helpful for those who may not have access to traditional in-person services. By utilizing these resources effectively, individuals and communities can work towards reducing the prevalence and impact of various health-related issues, such as mental health disorders, substance abuse, and domestic violence. By working together and leveraging the expertise and support of these resources, we can create healthier, safer, and more resilient communities for all.

Chapter 13: Body Image and Eating Disorders in Teenagers

- THE IMPACT OF SOCIETAL pressure on body image

Body image is a complex and multifaceted construct that encompasses an individual's perceptions, thoughts, and feelings about their own physical appearance. It is influenced by a variety of factors, including personal experiences, cultural norms, and societal pressures. One of the most significant influences on body image is societal pressure, which refers to the implicit and explicit messages from society about what is considered attractive or desirable.

Societal pressure on body image can take many forms, from media representations of idealized body types to peer pressure to conform to certain beauty standards. These messages can be harmful and detrimental to individuals' self-esteem and mental health, leading to body dissatisfaction, disordered eating behaviors, and even serious mental health conditions such as eating disorders. The constant barrage of images and messages promoting unrealistic beauty ideals can create a pervasive sense of inadequacy and insecurity, fueling feelings of shame and self-loathing.

One of the most pervasive forms of societal pressure on body image is the portrayal of thinness as the ideal standard of beauty. This is evident in the media, where celebrities and models are often celebrated for their slim and toned figures, while larger bodies are stigmatized and marginalized. This creates a narrow and exclusionary definition of beauty that is unattainable for the vast majority of people, leading to feelings of inadequacy and dissatisfaction with one's own body.

In addition to the pressure to conform to a certain body size or shape, individuals also face pressure to achieve other physical characteristics that are considered desirable by society. This can include having clear skin, straight teeth, and a youthful appearance. The proliferation of beauty standards in the media and popular culture can create a sense of competition and comparison among individuals, as they strive to meet these unrealistic and unattainable ideals.

Societal pressure on body image can also manifest in the form of weight stigma and discrimination. Larger bodies are often stigmatized and devalued in society, leading to negative stereotypes and prejudiced attitudes towards individuals who do not meet the thin ideal. This can contribute to low self-esteem and body dissatisfaction, as individuals internalize the negative messages about their bodies and begin to internalize shame and self-blame for their appearance.

It is important to recognize the damaging impact of societal pressure on body image and to work towards creating a more inclusive and accepting society. This can be done through promoting diverse representations of beauty in the media, challenging harmful beauty ideals, and advocating for body positivity and self-acceptance. By fostering a culture that celebrates diversity and individuality, we can help individuals to develop a more positive and healthy relationship with their bodies, free from the constraints of societal pressure.

- Common eating disorders in adolescents

Eating disorders are complex mental health conditions that can have serious physical and emotional consequences, particularly in adolescents. Adolescence is a period of rapid physical and emotional development, making it a vulnerable time for the development of eating disorders. This period of transition from childhood to adulthood is marked by increased pressure from peers, societal standards of beauty, and internal struggles with self-image and identity. As a result, it is not uncommon for adolescents to experience feelings of insecurity and low self-esteem, which may contribute to the development of disordered eating behaviors.

There are several common eating disorders that can affect adolescents, including anorexia nervosa, bulimia nervosa, and binge eating disorder.

Anorexia nervosa is characterized by a fear of gaining weight and a distorted body image, leading individuals to severely restrict their food intake. This can result in dangerously low body weight, malnutrition, and a range of physical health complications. Bulimia nervosa involves episodes of binge eating followed by purging behaviors, such as self-induced vomiting or excessive exercise, in an effort to compensate for the calories consumed. Binge eating disorder is characterized by episodes of uncontrollable eating, often leading to feelings of guilt and shame.

It is important to recognize the signs and symptoms of eating disorders in adolescents, as early intervention can greatly improve outcomes. Some common warning signs include sudden or extreme changes in weight, preoccupation with food, calories, and body image, frequent trips to the bathroom after meals, and social withdrawal. Additionally, adolescents with eating disorders may display mood swings, irritability, and a lack of energy or motivation. It is important for parents, teachers, and healthcare providers to be attentive to these warning signs and to approach the topic of eating disorders with sensitivity and compassion.

Treatment for eating disorders in adolescents typically involves a multidisciplinary approach, combining medical, nutritional, and psychological interventions. Medical evaluation is important to assess the physical health consequences of disordered eating, while nutritional counseling can help adolescents establish healthier eating habits and attitudes towards food. Psychological therapy, such as cognitive-behavioral therapy or family therapy, can address underlying emotional issues and help adolescents develop more positive coping mechanisms. In some cases, medication may be prescribed to manage symptoms of anxiety, depression, or other co-occurring mental health conditions.

It is crucial for adolescents with eating disorders to receive ongoing support from a team of healthcare professionals, as recovery can be a long and challenging process. Family involvement is also critical, as parents and caregivers play a key role in providing emotional support, monitoring progress, and helping adolescents navigate the challenges of recovery. It is important for families to communicate openly and honestly about the impact of the eating disorder on the individual and the family unit, while also fostering a supportive and non-judgmental environment. It is important for parents, teachers, and healthcare providers to be aware of the signs and symptoms of eating disorders in adolescents and to approach the topic with sensitivity and compassion. Early intervention and a multidisciplinary treatment approach are crucial for promoting recovery and long-term health and well-being in adolescents with eating disorders. By working together to provide support and encouragement, we can help adolescents overcome the challenges of eating disorders and lead fulfilling and healthy lives.

- Strategies for promoting a healthy body image and relationship with food

In today's society, the pressure to conform to narrow beauty standards can lead to unhealthy body image and disordered eating patterns. As such, it is crucial to develop strategies for promoting a healthy body image and a positive relationship with food. One approach is to focus on promoting overall health and well-being, rather than just striving for a specific body shape or size. Encouraging individuals to prioritize their physical and mental health, rather than conforming to societal ideals, can help foster a healthier relationship with their bodies.

Another important strategy is to promote body positivity and self-acceptance. It is essential to challenge negative societal norms and stereotypes around body image, and instead, promote acceptance and celebration of diverse body shapes and sizes. Encouraging individuals to embrace and love their bodies as they are can help improve self-esteem and reduce the prevalence of disordered eating behaviors.

Education is also a key component in promoting a healthy body image and relationship with food. Providing individuals with accurate and evidence-based information about nutrition, exercise, and body image can help dispel myths and misconceptions that contribute to negative feelings towards food and body. By empowering individuals with knowledge and skills to make informed choices about their health, they can develop a more positive and balanced relationship with food.

In addition to education, it is important to promote a balanced and intuitive approach to eating. Encouraging individuals to listen to their bodies' hunger and fullness cues, and to eat mindfully can help foster a healthier relationship with food. By focusing on nourishing their bodies with nutritious foods and enjoying treats in moderation, individuals can develop a more positive and sustainable approach to eating that supports their overall health and well-being.

Lastly, creating a supportive and inclusive environment is essential in promoting a healthy body image and relationship with food. Providing a safe space for individuals to discuss their feelings and experiences around body image and food can help reduce feelings of shame and isolation. Encouraging open and honest conversations about body image and food can help create a sense of community and support, which is essential in promoting positive attitudes towards food and body. By implementing these strategies, we can help individuals develop a more positive and sustainable relationship with their bodies and food, ultimately leading to improved health and well-being.

Chapter 14: Sexual Health and Relationships in Adolescence

- THE IMPORTANCE OF comprehensive sex education

Comprehensive sex education is a crucial aspect of education that provides young people with the tools and information they need to make informed decisions about their sexual health and well-being. By equipping students with accurate and age-appropriate information about sexuality, relationships, and reproductive health, comprehensive sex education helps individuals develop healthy attitudes and behaviors related to sex and relationships. It also plays a key role in preventing unintended pregnancies, sexually transmitted infections (STIs), and sexual violence.

One of the primary reasons why comprehensive sex education is so important is its emphasis on providing accurate and evidence-based information about sexual health. In many cases, young people may receive misinformation or incomplete information about sex and relationships from their peers, the media, or even family members. By ensuring that students have access to accurate and up-to-date information about topics such as contraception, consent, STIs, and reproductive anatomy, comprehensive sex education helps dispel myths and misconceptions and provides students with the knowledge they need to make informed decisions about their sexual health.

In addition to providing accurate information, comprehensive sex education also plays a crucial role in promoting healthy attitudes and behaviors related to sex and relationships. By discussing topics such as healthy relationships, communication, consent, and boundaries, comprehensive sex education helps young people develop the skills they need to navigate complex interpersonal dynamics and make healthy choices in their relationships. This can help prevent situations of coercion, manipulation, or abuse, and empower young people to prioritize their own well-being and safety in their relationships.

Furthermore, comprehensive sex education is important for promoting gender equality and addressing issues of power and privilege in relationships. By discussing topics such as gender roles, stereotypes, and norms, comprehensive sex education helps challenge harmful beliefs and practices that perpetuate inequality and discrimination. It also promotes respect and understanding for diverse gender identities and sexual orientations, creating an inclusive and supportive environment for all students to learn and grow.

Another key benefit of comprehensive sex education is its role in promoting sexual health and preventing negative outcomes such as unintended pregnancies and STIs. By providing students with information about contraception, safer sex practices, and the importance of regular testing and screenings, comprehensive sex education helps young people make responsible choices about their sexual health. This can have a significant impact on reducing rates of unintended pregnancies, STIs, and other negative outcomes associated with unprotected sex. By providing accurate information, promoting healthy attitudes and behaviors, challenging harmful beliefs and practices, and preventing negative outcomes, comprehensive sex education plays a crucial role in empowering young people to navigate the complexities of sex and relationships and lead healthy and fulfilling lives. It is essential that comprehensive sex education be integrated into school curricula and community programs to ensure that all young people have access to the information and support they need to make informed choices about their sexual health and well-being.

- Building healthy relationships and setting boundaries

Building healthy relationships and setting boundaries are essential aspects of maintaining positive and fulfilling connections with others. Whether it be in personal or professional settings, understanding how to establish and maintain boundaries is crucial for fostering trust, respect, and mutual understanding in relationships. By setting clear boundaries, individuals can communicate their needs, values, and limits effectively, while also respecting the boundaries of others. This process involves self-awareness, communication skills, and assertiveness, all of which are key components of building healthy relationships.

One of the first steps in building healthy relationships is understanding the importance of boundaries. Boundaries are the limits we set for ourselves in order to protect our physical, emotional, and mental well-being. They define what is acceptable and unacceptable behavior from others, as well as how we expect to be treated in various situations. Without boundaries, individuals may feel overwhelmed, stressed, or resentful, as they may not have clear guidelines for how to navigate interpersonal interactions. By setting boundaries, individuals can create a sense of safety, security, and autonomy in their relationships, which can ultimately lead to greater trust and intimacy with others.

In order to establish healthy boundaries, it is important to first reflect on one's own needs, values, and limits. This process involves self-awareness and self-reflection, as individuals must be able to identify what is important to them in their relationships and what they are willing to tolerate or not tolerate from others. By taking the time to understand their own boundaries, individuals can then communicate them effectively to others, which can prevent misunderstandings, conflicts, and resentment down the line. This self-awareness also allows individuals to prioritize their own well-being and set boundaries that are aligned with their values and goals.

Communication is another key aspect of setting boundaries and building healthy relationships. Effective communication involves expressing one's needs, feelings, and boundaries in a clear and assertive manner, while also listening to and respecting the boundaries of others. By being open and honest about their boundaries, individuals can prevent misunderstandings, conflicts, and hurt feelings in their relationships. This also allows for honest and authentic interactions with others, as both parties are able to express themselves openly and honestly without fear of judgment or retribution.

Setting boundaries also requires assertiveness, which involves standing up for one's own needs and rights while also respecting the needs and rights of others. Assertiveness is a skill that can be developed through practice and self-awareness, and it is essential for setting healthy boundaries in relationships.

By being assertive, individuals can communicate their boundaries confidently and respectfully, and they can also assert their rights and needs without being aggressive or passive. This allows for a balance of power and respect in relationships, as both parties are able to express themselves openly and assert their boundaries without fear of negative consequences.

In addition to communication and assertiveness, setting boundaries also involves enforcing consequences for violating those boundaries. This is an important aspect of maintaining healthy relationships, as it establishes accountability and respect between individuals. By enforcing consequences for boundary violations, individuals can demonstrate that their boundaries are important and non-negotiable, and that they are willing to uphold them in order to protect their well-being. This also helps to establish trust and respect in relationships, as both parties are held accountable for their actions and behaviors, and there are clear consequences for violating the established boundaries. By understanding the importance of boundaries, engaging in effective communication, practicing assertiveness, and enforcing consequences for boundary violations, individuals can create a sense of safety, security, and autonomy in their relationships. This process involves self-awareness, self-reflection, and emotional intelligence, all of which are key components of building and maintaining healthy relationships. By prioritizing their well-being and setting clear boundaries, individuals can cultivate positive and fulfilling connections with others, while also respecting the boundaries and needs of those around them.

- Resources for navigating sexual health issues

Navigating sexual health issues can be a complex and sometimes overwhelming task. However, there are a variety of resources available to help individuals navigate these issues in a safe and informed manner. One of the most important resources for addressing sexual health concerns is healthcare providers. Whether it be a primary care physician, gynecologist, or urologist, healthcare providers play a critical role in providing guidance, information, and support related to sexual health.

Another valuable resource for navigating sexual health issues is sexual health clinics. These clinics specialize in providing services related to sexual health, including testing for sexually transmitted infections (STIs), contraception counseling, and general sexual health education. Sexual health clinics often offer a safe and confidential environment for individuals to discuss their concerns and receive the care they need.

In addition to healthcare providers and sexual health clinics, there are also a variety of online resources available to help individuals navigate sexual health issues. Websites such as Planned Parenthood and the Centers for Disease Control and Prevention (CDC) offer a wealth of information on topics such as contraception, STIs, and sexual health education. These online resources can be a valuable tool for individuals who may not feel comfortable discussing their concerns in person or who are unable to access traditional healthcare services.

Furthermore, community-based organizations and NGOs can also be valuable resources for navigating sexual health issues. These organizations often offer support groups, educational workshops, and other services aimed at promoting sexual health and well-being. By connecting with these organizations, individuals can gain access to a network of support and information that can help them address their sexual health concerns in a positive and empowering way. Healthcare providers, sexual health clinics, online resources, and community-based organizations all play a critical role in supporting individuals in their journey towards sexual health and well-being. By utilizing these resources and seeking out the support they offer, individuals can take control of their sexual health and make informed decisions that promote their overall well-being.

Chapter 15: Peer Conflict and Bullying in Adolescence

- THE IMPACT OF PEER conflict and bullying on teenage well-being

Peer conflict and bullying are pervasive issues that have a significant impact on the well-being of teenagers. Adolescence is a crucial stage in a person's development, as individuals begin to form their sense of identity and establish relationships with their peers. When conflicts arise between peers or when a teenager is subjected to bullying, the consequences can be far-reaching and detrimental. Research has shown that peer conflict and bullying can have negative effects on various aspects of teenage well-being, including mental health, social relationships, academic performance, and overall self-esteem.

One of the most concerning effects of peer conflict and bullying on teenage well-being is the impact on mental health. Adolescents who experience conflict with their peers or are victims of bullying are at an increased risk of developing mental health issues such as anxiety, depression, and low self-esteem. The constant stress and pressure of dealing with peer conflict or bullying can take a toll on a teenager's emotional well-being, leading to feelings of isolation, helplessness, and worthlessness. These negative emotions can in turn affect their ability to concentrate in school, participate in social activities, and maintain healthy relationships with their peers and family members.

Furthermore, peer conflict and bullying can have a significant impact on a teenager's social relationships. Adolescents who are involved in ongoing conflicts with their peers may find it difficult to establish and maintain positive relationships with others. They may become withdrawn, isolated, or defensive, making it challenging for them to form meaningful connections with their peers. In cases of bullying, victims may experience social exclusion, humiliation, and rejection from their peers, leading to feelings of loneliness and alienation. These negative social experiences can further exacerbate the mental health issues that teenagers may be facing, creating a cycle of isolation and distress that can be difficult to break.

In addition to its effects on mental health and social relationships, peer conflict and bullying can also impact a teenager's academic performance. Adolescents who are dealing with conflicts or bullying at school may struggle to focus on their studies, leading to a decline in academic performance and achievement. The stress and anxiety caused by peer conflict and bullying can interfere with a teenager's ability to concentrate, retain information, and complete assignments, ultimately affecting their grades and overall academic success. In severe cases, teenagers may even resort to skipping school, dropping out entirely, or engaging in risky behaviors as a way to cope with the challenges they are facing.

Moreover, peer conflict and bullying can have a detrimental effect on a teenager's self-esteem and sense of self-worth. Adolescents who are victims of bullying may internalize the negative messages and beliefs that they are unworthy, unlikable, or inferior to their peers. This can result in a loss of self-confidence, self-esteem, and self-respect, leading to feelings of inadequacy and worthlessness. These negative beliefs and emotions can manifest in various ways, such as engaging in self-destructive behaviors, developing an unhealthy body image, or experiencing feelings of shame and guilt. It is essential for teenagers who are experiencing peer conflict or bullying to seek support from trusted adults, such as parents, teachers, or mental health professionals, to help them navigate these challenging experiences and rebuild their sense of self-worth. It is crucial for parents, educators, and policymakers to address these issues proactively, by promoting a positive and inclusive school environment, providing resources and support for teenagers who are experiencing peer conflict or bullying, and educating both students and adults on the harmful effects of these behaviors. By creating a safe and supportive community for teenagers to thrive in, we can help mitigate the negative impact of peer conflict and bullying on their well-being and foster a healthy and positive environment for all.

- Strategies for responding to and preventing bullying

Bullying is a pervasive issue that affects individuals of all ages and backgrounds. It can have a profound impact on the mental health and well-being of those who experience it, leading to feelings of isolation, anxiety, and depression. In some cases, bullying can even result in physical harm or long-term psychological trauma. As such, it is essential for individuals, communities, and institutions to take proactive measures to respond to and prevent bullying.

One of the most effective strategies for responding to bullying is to create a culture of empathy and inclusion within schools, workplaces, and other social settings. By fostering an environment where kindness and respect are valued, individuals are more likely to feel supported and protected from bullying behavior. This can be achieved through promoting positive relationships, teaching conflict resolution skills, and encouraging bystanders to speak up when they witness bullying. Additionally, providing resources and support for those who have experienced bullying can help them cope with the effects of the trauma and rebuild their self-confidence.

In addition to creating a supportive environment, it is crucial to establish clear policies and procedures for addressing bullying incidents. Schools, workplaces, and other organizations should have comprehensive anti-bullying policies in place that outline what constitutes bullying, the consequences for engaging in such behavior, and the steps that will be taken to address reports of bullying. These policies should be regularly communicated to individuals within the organization and consistently enforced to send a clear message that bullying will not be tolerated.

Furthermore, education and awareness are key components of any bullying prevention strategy. By teaching individuals about the different forms of bullying, the impact it can have on victims, and the role they can play in preventing bullying, we can empower people to take action and be part of the solution. This can be done through workshops, training programs, and informational campaigns that raise awareness about the issue of bullying and provide individuals with the tools they need to intervene effectively.

Another important aspect of preventing bullying is to address the underlying causes of the behavior. Research has shown that individuals who engage in bullying often do so because they themselves have experienced trauma or abuse, lack social skills, or have low self-esteem. By addressing these root causes through therapy, counseling, or other interventions, we can help individuals develop healthier coping mechanisms and reduce the likelihood of them engaging in bullying behavior.

Ultimately, the key to responding to and preventing bullying lies in creating a culture of respect, empathy, and inclusivity. By fostering positive relationships, establishing clear policies, providing education and awareness, and addressing the underlying causes of bullying, we can create a safer and more supportive environment for all individuals. Together, we can work towards a society where bullying is no longer a pervasive issue, and where everyone can feel safe and valued.

- Building resilience and developing conflict resolution skills

Resilience is a critical skill that helps individuals to adapt and cope with adversity and challenges in their personal and professional lives. It is essential for navigating through difficult situations, such as conflicts in the workplace or at home. Building resilience involves developing a mindset that enables individuals to bounce back from setbacks and setbacks quickly and effectively. This can be achieved through various strategies, such as fostering positive thinking, cultivating emotional intelligence, and practicing self-care.

One key aspect of building resilience is developing conflict resolution skills. Conflict resolution is the process of managing and resolving disagreements or disputes in a constructive manner. It involves communication, negotiation, and problem-solving techniques to find mutually acceptable solutions. Developing effective conflict resolution skills can help individuals to navigate conflicts in a productive way, rather than letting them escalate and cause further harm.

There are several steps that individuals can take to build resilience and develop conflict resolution skills. One important aspect is to cultivate self-awareness and self-regulation. This involves being aware of one's emotions, thoughts, and behaviors, and developing the ability to manage them effectively. By being able to recognize and regulate their emotions, individuals can respond to conflicts in a calm and rational manner, rather than reacting impulsively or defensively.

Another key step in building resilience and developing conflict resolution skills is to improve communication and interpersonal skills. Effective communication is essential for resolving conflicts, as it allows individuals to express their thoughts and feelings clearly and assertively, while also listening actively and empathetically to others' perspectives. By improving their communication skills, individuals can enhance their ability to communicate effectively in difficult situations and find common ground with others.

Furthermore, developing problem-solving and negotiation skills is crucial for building resilience and resolving conflicts. Problem-solving skills involve identifying and analyzing the root causes of conflicts, brainstorming potential solutions, and implementing strategies to address them effectively. Negotiation skills, on the other hand, involve finding compromises and reaching agreements that are acceptable to all parties involved. By honing their problem-solving and negotiation skills, individuals can approach conflicts with a collaborative mindset and work towards finding win-win solutions.

In addition to these steps, practicing self-care and building a strong support network can also help individuals to build resilience and develop conflict resolution skills. Self-care involves taking care of one's physical, emotional, and mental well-being, through activities such as exercise, mindfulness, and relaxation techniques. By taking care of themselves, individuals can build emotional resilience and have the energy and resources to deal with conflicts more effectively.

Moreover, having a strong support network of friends, family, and colleagues can provide individuals with the emotional support and perspective they need to navigate conflicts and challenges. By seeking guidance and advice from trusted individuals, individuals can gain new insights and strategies for managing conflicts and resolving disputes. Building a support network also helps individuals to feel connected and supported, which can boost their resilience and confidence in dealing with difficult situations. By cultivating self-awareness, improving communication and interpersonal skills, and honing problem-solving and negotiation skills, individuals can build the resilience and confidence they need to face conflicts in a constructive and productive manner. Additionally, practicing self-care and building a strong support network can provide individuals with the emotional support and resources they need to cope with challenges effectively. By taking proactive steps to build resilience and develop conflict resolution skills, individuals can enhance their ability to handle conflicts and setbacks with grace and resilience.

Chapter 16: Cultural Influences on Teenage Development

- THE ROLE OF CULTURE in shaping adolescent identity

Adolescence is a critical period of development marked by physical, cognitive, emotional, and social changes. During this time, individuals begin to explore and define their identities. One factor that plays a significant role in shaping adolescent identity is culture. Culture refers to the beliefs, values, norms, customs, traditions, and practices shared by a group of people.

Culture influences adolescent identity in several ways. Firstly, culture provides adolescents with a sense of belonging and connection to their community. By participating in cultural practices and traditions, adolescents develop a sense of cultural identity and pride. For example, a teenager who belongs to a religious community may draw strength and support from their faith during challenging times. Cultural identity helps adolescents navigate their way through the complex process of identity development, providing them with a sense of continuity and stability.

Secondly, culture shapes adolescent identity by influencing their values and beliefs. Adolescents internalize the beliefs and values of their culture, which influence their attitudes, behaviors, and decision-making processes. For example, in some cultures, family values are highly emphasized, and adolescents are expected to prioritize family obligations over personal desires. In contrast, in other cultures, individualism and independence are valued, and adolescents are encouraged to pursue their own goals and ambitions. These cultural differences impact how adolescents perceive themselves and their place in the world.

Moreover, culture impacts adolescent identity through socialization processes. Adolescents are socialized into their culture through interactions with family members, peers, schools, media, and other social institutions. These socialization experiences shape their attitudes, beliefs, behaviors, and identities. For example, adolescents may adopt the fashion trends, music preferences, language, and social norms of their culture, which help them establish a sense of identity and belonging. Cultural socialization also teaches adolescents about their roles, responsibilities, and expectations within their cultural group.

Furthermore, culture influences adolescent identity by shaping their relationships and social networks. Adolescents often form relationships with individuals who share similar cultural backgrounds, values, and interests. These relationships provide adolescents with support, validation, and a sense of community. For example, belonging to a cultural or ethnic group may provide adolescents with a sense of pride, shared history, and solidarity. These relationships help adolescents develop a sense of identity and belonging within their cultural context.

In addition, culture impacts adolescent identity through the process of acculturation. Acculturation refers to the process of adapting to a new culture while retaining aspects of one's own culture. Adolescents who are part of immigrant families, for example, often navigate between their original cultural identity and the dominant culture of their new country. This process can be challenging as adolescents may experience conflicts, confusion, and identity negotiation. However, acculturation can also be a source of strength and resilience for adolescents, as they develop a bicultural identity that incorporates elements of both cultures. It provides adolescents with a sense of belonging, influences their values and beliefs, shapes their socialization experiences, impacts their relationships and social networks, and influences the process of acculturation. Understanding the role of culture in adolescent identity development is essential for educators, parents, and policymakers to support adolescents in navigating this critical period of growth and development. By fostering a positive cultural identity, providing opportunities for adolescents to explore and express their cultural heritage, and promoting intercultural understanding and respect, we can help adolescents develop a strong and resilient sense of identity that integrates their cultural background with their individual uniqueness.

- The impact of intersectionality on teenage experiences

Intersectionality is a concept that defines the complex ways in which various social categories such as race, gender, class, sexuality, and ability intersect and interact to create unique experiences and disadvantages for individuals. This concept was originally coined by legal scholar Kimberlé Crenshaw in the late 1980s to address the ways in which black women were marginalized in both feminist and anti-racist movements. Since then, intersectionality has become a crucial framework for understanding the multiple dimensions of oppression and privilege that individuals may experience.

When it comes to teenage experiences, intersectionality plays a significant role in shaping how young people navigate their identities and social environments. Teenagers are at a critical stage of development where they are exploring and forming their identities, and the intersection of various social categories can have a profound impact on their experiences. For example, a teenage girl who belongs to a racial minority group may face unique challenges that are different from her white peers, such as discrimination and stereotyping based on her race. Similarly, a teenage boy who identifies as LGBTQ+ may experience discrimination and isolation due to his sexual orientation or gender identity.

Intersectionality also impacts how teenagers access resources and opportunities in society. For instance, a teenage girl from a low-income family may face barriers to education and employment due to her socioeconomic status, which intersects with her gender and race. This can result in limited access to quality education, healthcare, and other essential services, further exacerbating existing inequalities. In contrast, a teenage boy from a privileged background may have more opportunities and advantages due to his social position, which intersects with his gender and race in a different way.

Moreover, intersectionality influences how teenagers navigate relationships and social dynamics in their peer groups and communities. Adolescence is a time when young people are forming friendships, developing romantic relationships, and exploring their sexual identities. The intersection of social categories such as race, gender, and sexuality can impact how teenagers are perceived by their peers and how they navigate social interactions. For example, a teenage girl who identifies as transgender may face discrimination and bullying from her peers due to her gender identity, which intersects with her age and sexuality. Understanding the intersectional nature of oppression and privilege is crucial for creating inclusive and supportive environments for teenagers to thrive and reach their full potential. By recognizing and addressing the overlapping and intersecting systems of power and discrimination that shape teenage experiences, we can work towards creating a more equitable and just society for all young people.

- Strategies for promoting cultural understanding and inclusivity

Promoting cultural understanding and inclusivity is crucial in today's diverse and interconnected world. In order to build bridges across different cultures and foster a sense of belonging for all individuals, it is essential to implement strategies that prioritize mutual respect, empathy, and open-mindedness. By recognizing the unique perspectives and experiences of various cultural groups, we can create a more inclusive and harmonious society where everyone feels valued and accepted.

One of the key strategies for promoting cultural understanding and inclusivity is through education and awareness. By providing individuals with opportunities to learn about different cultures, traditions, and beliefs, we can help break down stereotypes and misconceptions that may lead to discrimination and prejudice. Educational initiatives such as multicultural events, workshops, and diversity training programs can help foster cultural awareness and appreciation among individuals of all ages. By encouraging intercultural dialogue and exchange, we can create a more inclusive and respectful environment where diversity is celebrated.

Another important strategy for promoting cultural understanding and inclusivity is through effective communication and collaboration. By actively engaging with individuals from different cultural backgrounds, we can build relationships based on trust, empathy, and understanding. This can be accomplished through initiatives such as cultural exchange programs, community events, and collaborative projects that bring people together to work towards a common goal. By fostering a sense of shared humanity and collective responsibility, we can create a more inclusive and supportive community where everyone feels welcome and valued.

In addition to education and communication, it is also important to address systemic barriers and inequities that may limit access and opportunities for individuals from diverse cultural backgrounds. This can include advocating for policies and practices that promote diversity, equity, and inclusion in various sectors such as education, healthcare, employment, and housing. By working towards removing structural barriers and creating more inclusive and equitable systems, we can ensure that all individuals have equal opportunities to succeed and thrive in a multicultural society.

Furthermore, it is important to promote cultural understanding and inclusivity through the arts and media. By showcasing diverse cultural perspectives and narratives through literature, music, art, film, and other forms of creative expression, we can help challenge stereotypes and promote empathy and understanding among people from different cultural backgrounds. By supporting and celebrating the contributions of artists and creators from diverse backgrounds, we can create a more inclusive and culturally rich society that reflects the diversity of our global community. By implementing strategies that prioritize education, communication, collaboration, and advocacy, we can create a more inclusive and respectful environment where everyone feels valued and accepted. By working together to celebrate and embrace our differences, we can build bridges across cultures and create a more inclusive and equitable world for all individuals.

Chapter 17: Gender and Sexuality in Adolescence

- THE EXPLORATION OF gender and sexuality in teenage development

Adolescence is a crucial period in a person's life, marked by profound physical, emotional, and psychological changes. One of the key aspects of teenage development is the exploration of gender and sexuality. During this time, individuals begin to form their identities and understand their place in society, including how they identify in terms of gender and sexuality. This process can be complex and challenging, as teens navigate societal expectations, personal beliefs, and emerging desires.

Gender identity refers to an individual's internal sense of their own gender, which may or may not align with the sex they were assigned at birth. For many teenagers, this is a time of questioning and self-discovery as they come to terms with their gender identity. Some teens may identify as cisgender, meaning their gender identity matches the sex they were assigned at birth. Others may identify as transgender, nonbinary, or genderqueer, among other identities. It is important for adults and peers to support and validate teenagers in their exploration of gender identity, as this can have a profound impact on their mental health and well-being.

Sexuality, on the other hand, refers to an individual's sexual orientation or attraction to others. Teenagers may begin to explore their sexuality during adolescence, as they develop romantic and sexual feelings towards others. It is important for teenagers to feel empowered to explore and understand their sexuality in a safe and supportive environment. This may involve having open and honest conversations with trusted adults, seeking out resources and information, and connecting with peers who share similar experiences.

There are many factors that can influence how teenagers explore and understand their gender and sexuality. Society's norms and expectations around gender and sexuality can play a significant role in shaping teenagers' beliefs and attitudes. For example, traditional gender roles may limit teenagers' options for self-expression and exploration. Additionally, societal stigma and discrimination towards LGBTQ+ individuals can create barriers for teenagers who are exploring their gender and sexuality.

Family dynamics also play a crucial role in how teenagers navigate their gender and sexuality. Supportive and accepting families can provide a safe and nurturing environment for teenagers to explore their identities. On the other hand, families that are unsupportive or hostile towards LGBTQ+ individuals can create additional challenges for teenagers. It is important for families to have open and honest conversations about gender and sexuality, and to provide unconditional love and support for their children as they navigate this aspect of their development.

Peers and social networks can also have a significant influence on how teenagers explore their gender and sexuality. Friends and classmates can provide a sense of belonging and acceptance for teenagers who may be questioning their identities. However, peer pressure and social norms can also create challenges for teenagers who are exploring their gender and sexuality. It is important for teenagers to surround themselves with supportive and understanding peers who respect their individuality and choices. During adolescence, individuals begin to form their identities and understand their place in society, including how they identify in terms of gender and sexuality. It is important for adults, families, and peers to support and validate teenagers in their exploration of gender and sexuality, creating a safe and inclusive environment for self-discovery. By fostering open and honest conversations, providing resources and information, and offering unconditional love and support, we can help teenagers navigate this important aspect of their development with confidence and self-acceptance.

- Promoting LGBTQ+ inclusivity and acceptance

Promoting LGBTQ+ inclusivity and acceptance is a crucial aspect of creating a more inclusive and diverse society. The LGBTQ+ community comprises individuals who identify as lesbian, gay, bisexual, transgender, queer, and others who do not conform to traditional gender and sexual orientation norms. Throughout history, LGBTQ+ individuals have faced discrimination, prejudice, and marginalization due to their identities. It is essential to recognize the unique challenges that LGBTQ+ individuals face and work towards fostering a more inclusive and accepting environment for all individuals, regardless of their sexual orientation or gender identity.

One of the first steps in promoting LGBTQ+ inclusivity and acceptance is to educate oneself about LGBTQ+ identities, experiences, and issues. This includes understanding the terminology used within the LGBTQ+ community, such as the difference between sexual orientation and gender identity, as well as the various identities that fall under the LGBTQ+ umbrella. It is also essential to familiarize oneself with the challenges that LGBTQ+ individuals face, such as discrimination, violence, and mental health disparities. By educating oneself about LGBTQ+ identities and experiences, individuals can become more empathetic and understanding towards LGBTQ+ individuals and work towards creating a more inclusive environment.

Additionally, promoting LGBTQ+ inclusivity and acceptance involves challenging stereotypes and misconceptions about LGBTQ+ individuals. Stereotypes such as assuming that all LGBTQ+ individuals are promiscuous, that being LGBTQ+ is a choice, or that LGBTQ+ individuals are not fit to be parents perpetuate negative attitudes towards the community. By challenging these stereotypes and misconceptions, individuals can help create a more accepting and inclusive environment for LGBTQ+ individuals. This can be done by speaking out against discriminatory language and behavior, as well as actively promoting positive representations of LGBTQ+ individuals in the media and society.

Another crucial aspect of promoting LGBTQ+ inclusivity and acceptance is advocating for LGBTQ+ rights and equality. LGBTQ+ individuals continue to face discrimination and marginalization in various areas of life, including employment, housing, healthcare, and education. By advocating for policies and laws that protect LGBTQ+ rights, individuals can help create a more equitable society for all individuals, regardless of their sexual orientation or gender identity. This includes supporting anti-discrimination laws, marriage equality, and transgender rights, as well as promoting LGBTQ+ representation in politics and leadership positions.

Furthermore, promoting LGBTQ+ inclusivity and acceptance involves creating safe and supportive spaces for LGBTQ+ individuals to express themselves and be their authentic selves. This can be done by promoting LGBTQ+-friendly businesses, organizations, and events, as well as ensuring that LGBTQ+ individuals have access to resources and support services. By creating inclusive and welcoming spaces for LGBTQ+ individuals, individuals can help foster a sense of belonging and acceptance within the community. This can also help combat feelings of isolation and loneliness that LGBTQ+ individuals may experience due to societal stigma and discrimination. By educating oneself, challenging stereotypes, advocating for LGBTQ+ rights, and creating safe and supportive spaces, individuals can help create a more accepting environment for LGBTQ+ individuals. It is important to recognize the unique challenges that LGBTQ+ individuals face and work towards creating a society where all individuals can live authentically and free from discrimination and prejudice. By promoting LGBTQ+ inclusivity and acceptance, individuals can contribute to a more equitable and just society for all.

- Resources for supporting gender and sexual diversity

Gender and sexual diversity are important aspects of human identity that have gained increasing recognition and acceptance in recent years. However, individuals who identify as gender and sexually diverse often face unique challenges and barriers in society. It is crucial for communities and organizations to provide support and resources to help these individuals navigate these challenges and live authentically.

One key resource for supporting gender and sexual diversity is access to inclusive healthcare services. Healthcare providers play a critical role in ensuring that individuals of all gender identities and sexual orientations receive the care and support they need. This includes providing culturally competent care, offering resources for gender-affirming treatments, and creating a safe and welcoming environment for all patients. It is important for healthcare providers to educate themselves on the specific needs and experiences of gender and sexually diverse individuals in order to provide effective and compassionate care.

Additionally, mental health support is vital for individuals who identify as gender and sexually diverse. Many individuals in this community face higher rates of mental health issues such as depression, anxiety, and suicidality due to societal stigma and discrimination. Access to affirming and inclusive mental health services can make a significant difference in the well-being of these individuals. It is essential for mental health providers to create a space that is free from judgment and bias, and to offer specialized support for the unique challenges faced by gender and sexually diverse individuals.

Another important resource for supporting gender and sexual diversity is access to social support networks and community organizations. These groups can provide a sense of belonging and connection for individuals who may feel isolated or marginalized by society. Community organizations often offer a range of services and programs, such as support groups, advocacy initiatives, and educational workshops, to help empower and uplift gender and sexually diverse individuals. By connecting with others who share similar experiences, individuals can find validation, support, and solidarity in a world that may not always be accepting of their identities.

Education and awareness are also crucial resources for supporting gender and sexual diversity. It is essential for individuals, communities, and organizations to educate themselves on the diverse experiences and needs of gender and sexually diverse individuals in order to foster understanding and acceptance. This can involve training programs, workshops, and educational resources that raise awareness of issues such as gender identity, sexual orientation, and intersectionality. By promoting education and awareness, we can help create a more inclusive and supportive environment for all individuals, regardless of their gender or sexual orientation.

Legal protections and advocacy efforts are another important resource for supporting gender and sexual diversity. Many individuals in this community face discrimination and stigma in various areas of their lives, such as employment, housing, and healthcare. Legal protections, such as anti-discrimination laws and policies, can help safeguard the rights and well-being of gender and sexually diverse individuals. Advocacy efforts, such as lobbying for inclusive policies and working to dismantle systems of oppression, can also create lasting change and promote greater equity and justice for all individuals. By advocating for legal protections and supporting advocacy efforts, we can help create a more just and equitable society for everyone. From inclusive healthcare services and mental health support to social networks and education initiatives, these resources play a crucial role in helping individuals navigate the challenges they may face and live authentically. By promoting understanding, acceptance, and advocacy, we can create a more inclusive and supportive environment for all individuals, regardless of their gender or sexual orientation. It is important for communities and organizations to come together to provide these resources and support gender and sexual diversity in order to create a more equitable and just society for all.

Chapter 18: Positive Youth Development and Community Engagement

- THE IMPORTANCE OF community connections for teenage well-being

Community connections play a crucial role in the well-being of teenagers. Adolescence is a period of immense change, growth, and development, both physically and emotionally. During this critical time, teenagers are often seeking to establish their identity, develop relationships, and navigate the challenges of school, family, and society. In this context, community connections provide teenagers with a sense of belonging, support, and opportunities for growth and development.

One of the key aspects of community connections for teenage well-being is the sense of belonging that they provide. Teenagers are at a stage in their lives where they are developing a strong sense of identity and self-esteem. Being part of a community, whether it be a school, sports team, club, or neighborhood group, can help teenagers feel like they belong and are valued by others. This sense of belonging can be particularly important for teenagers who may feel isolated or alienated, as it can provide them with a sense of connection and support that they may not find elsewhere.

Furthermore, community connections can also provide teenagers with valuable social support. Teenagers who have strong connections to their community are more likely to have friends, mentors, and other supportive relationships that can help them navigate the challenges of adolescence. These relationships can provide teenagers with emotional support, guidance, and encouragement, helping them to cope with stress, build resilience, and develop healthy coping mechanisms. In addition, community connections can also provide teenagers with opportunities for social engagement, collaboration, and teamwork, which can help them develop important social skills, such as communication, empathy, and conflict resolution.

Community connections can also play a significant role in the academic success of teenagers. Research has shown that teenagers who are actively engaged in their communities, whether through extracurricular activities, volunteer work, or other forms of community involvement, tend to have higher levels of academic achievement and motivation. This is because community connections can provide teenagers with a sense of purpose, motivation, and accountability, as well as access to resources, support, and opportunities for learning and growth. By engaging with their communities, teenagers can develop important skills, such as time management, organization, and teamwork, that can help them succeed academically and prepare for future success.

In addition to the tangible benefits of community connections, such as social support and academic success, there is also a growing body of research that suggests that community connections can have a positive impact on the mental health and well-being of teenagers. Adolescence is a time of increased vulnerability to mental health issues, such as anxiety, depression, and stress, and teenagers who lack strong community connections may be at greater risk of developing these issues. On the other hand, teenagers who have strong community connections are more likely to have positive mental health outcomes, including higher levels of self-esteem, resilience, and overall well-being. This is because community connections can provide teenagers with a sense of belonging, social support, and purpose, all of which are important predictors of mental health and well-being. By providing a sense of belonging, social support, and opportunities for growth and development, community connections can help teenagers navigate the challenges of adolescence, develop important social skills, succeed academically, and maintain positive mental health outcomes. As such, it is important for parents, educators, and community leaders to support and encourage teenagers to build and maintain strong connections to their communities, as this can have a lasting impact on their well-being and success in life.

- Strategies for promoting social responsibility and civic engagement

Social responsibility and civic engagement are essential components of a thriving society. When individuals and organizations actively participate in activities that benefit the greater good, they contribute to the overall well-being of their communities. However, promoting social responsibility and civic engagement requires a concerted effort and strategic approach. In this article, we will explore various strategies that can be employed to encourage individuals and organizations to take on a more active role in their communities and society as a whole.

One of the key strategies for promoting social responsibility and civic engagement is education. By educating individuals about the importance of these concepts and the impact they can have on society, we can empower them to take action and make a positive difference. This can be done through formal education programs in schools and universities, as well as through public awareness campaigns and workshops. By providing individuals with the knowledge and tools they need to engage with their communities, we can inspire them to become more socially responsible and civically engaged citizens.

Another important strategy for promoting social responsibility and civic engagement is collaboration. By partnering with other organizations, businesses, and government agencies, we can amplify our efforts and reach a broader audience. Collaborative initiatives can take many forms, from joint community service projects to co-sponsored events and campaigns. By working together towards a common goal, we can leverage our collective resources and expertise to effect real change in our communities.

In addition to education and collaboration, incentives can also be a powerful tool for promoting social responsibility and civic engagement. By offering rewards and recognition for individuals and organizations that demonstrate exemplary social responsibility, we can create a culture of accountability and encourage others to follow suit. Incentives can take many forms, from awards and certificates to tax breaks and other financial incentives. By incentivizing social responsibility, we can motivate individuals and organizations to prioritize community engagement and make a meaningful impact on society.

Furthermore, technology can play a crucial role in promoting social responsibility and civic engagement. With the widespread use of social media and other digital platforms, individuals and organizations have unprecedented opportunities to connect with one another and mobilize for change. By harnessing the power of technology, we can reach a larger audience, raise awareness about important social issues, and coordinate collective action. From online petitions and crowdfunding campaigns to virtual volunteering opportunities, technology can empower individuals to make a difference in their communities and the world at large.

Lastly, creating opportunities for meaningful engagement is essential for promoting social responsibility and civic engagement. By providing individuals and organizations with tangible ways to get involved in their communities, we can ensure that their efforts have a real and lasting impact. This can include volunteering opportunities, community service projects, and advocacy campaigns. By offering a variety of ways for individuals to contribute to society, we can cater to different interests and skill sets, ensuring that everyone has a chance to make a meaningful contribution. By employing strategies such as education, collaboration, incentives, technology, and creating opportunities for meaningful engagement, we can inspire individuals and organizations to take an active role in shaping their communities and making a positive impact on the world. Through these collective efforts, we can work towards a more socially responsible and civically engaged society for future generations.

- Building skills and passions through extracurricular activities

Extracurricular activities play a crucial role in helping individuals build skills and explore their passions outside of the traditional classroom setting. Whether it be sports, arts, academic clubs, or community service, extracurricular activities offer numerous benefits that contribute to a well-rounded education and help individuals thrive in various aspects of their lives.

One of the key advantages of participating in extracurricular activities is the opportunity to build and hone a diverse set of skills. Through engaging in activities such as student government, debate club, or volunteering, students can develop essential skills such as teamwork, leadership, communication, time management, and problem-solving. These skills are not only valuable in a school setting but also in the workforce and everyday life. For instance, being a member of a sports team teaches individuals how to work collaboratively towards a common goal, while joining the school newspaper club can enhance writing and journalism skills. By actively participating in extracurricular activities, individuals can acquire a wide range of transferable skills that will serve them well in a variety of contexts.

Moreover, extracurricular activities provide a platform for individuals to explore their passions and interests in a supportive and nurturing environment. For many students, school can be a highly structured and academic-focused environment, leaving little room for personal exploration and self-discovery. Extracurricular activities offer a space where individuals can pursue their passions, whether it be through music, art, dance, or science. By engaging in activities that align with their interests, students can cultivate a sense of purpose, motivation, and fulfillment.

In addition to developing skills and exploring passions, extracurricular activities also provide individuals with valuable networking opportunities and real-world experiences. Many extracurricular activities involve working closely with peers, teachers, mentors, and community members, allowing students to build relationships and establish connections that can be beneficial in the future. For example, participating in a business club may lead to networking opportunities with professionals in the field, while volunteering at a local charity organization can help individuals gain hands-on experience and a deeper understanding of social issues. These experiences not only contribute to personal growth but also help individuals cultivate a strong support system and professional network that can assist them in their future endeavors.

Furthermore, engaging in extracurricular activities can help individuals stand out in college applications, job interviews, and other competitive settings. Admissions officers and employers often look for candidates who demonstrate a well-rounded skill set, a passion for learning, and a commitment to personal development. By showcasing their involvement in extracurricular activities, individuals can highlight their diverse interests, leadership abilities, and dedication to excellence. This can give them a competitive edge and set them apart from other candidates who may have similar academic achievements but lack the same level of extracurricular involvement. In today's competitive academic and professional landscape, having a strong extracurricular profile can make a significant difference in one's opportunities for success. By engaging in a diverse range of activities, individuals can build valuable skills, explore their passions, expand their networks, and distinguish themselves in competitive settings. Whether it be through sports, arts, clubs, or volunteer work, extracurricular activities provide a valuable platform for individuals to develop their talents, pursue their interests, and make a positive impact on their communities. It is important for students to actively seek out and participate in extracurricular activities that align with their interests and goals, as these experiences can have a lasting impact on their personal and professional development.

Chapter 19: Challenges and Opportunities for Youth in Society

- RECOGNIZING THE UNIQUE challenges faced by teenagers in today's world

Adolescence is a critical stage of development that presents a myriad of challenges for individuals as they navigate the complexities of the modern world. Teenagers today are faced with unique obstacles that previous generations did not have to contend with, making their journey to adulthood a particularly challenging one. From the pressures of social media and cyberbullying to the increasing academic demands and expectations placed upon them, teenagers today are bombarded with stimuli that can have a profound impact on their mental health and overall well-being.

One of the most prominent challenges facing teenagers in today's world is the proliferation of social media and its effect on their self-esteem and mental health. Platforms like Instagram, Snapchat, and TikTok have become integral parts of many teenagers' lives, providing them with a constant stream of curated images and videos that often promote unrealistic standards of beauty and success. This can lead to feelings of inadequacy and comparison, as teenagers struggle to measure up to the seemingly perfect lives portrayed on social media. Additionally, the prevalence of cyberbullying on these platforms can further exacerbate feelings of isolation and anxiety, making it difficult for teenagers to develop a healthy sense of self-worth.

In addition to the pressures of social media, teenagers today also face increasing academic demands that can contribute to stress and burnout. With college admissions becoming more competitive than ever, teenagers are under tremendous pressure to excel academically and participate in a wide range of extracurricular activities in order to stand out to admissions committees. This can lead to a culture of perfectionism and overachievement, where teenagers feel the need to constantly push themselves to their limits in order to succeed. As a result, many teenagers experience high levels of stress and anxiety, which can have long-term consequences on their mental and physical health.

Furthermore, teenagers today are also grappling with the effects of a rapidly changing world, including environmental challenges, political unrest, and economic uncertainty. Issues like climate change, social inequality, and global pandemics can feel overwhelming for teenagers, who are still in the process of forming their identities and understanding their place in the world. This sense of uncertainty and instability can contribute to feelings of helplessness and despair, as teenagers struggle to make sense of a world that often seems chaotic and unpredictable. Additionally, the pervasive use of technology and screen time can further isolate teenagers from real-world connections and experiences, making it difficult for them to develop the interpersonal skills necessary to navigate the challenges of adulthood.

Despite these numerous challenges, it is important to recognize the resilience and strength of teenagers in today's world. Many teenagers are actively working to address these issues through activism, advocacy, and community engagement, demonstrating a powerful commitment to creating positive change in their communities and the world at large. By recognizing and supporting the unique challenges faced by teenagers today, we can work together to create a more inclusive and supportive environment that empowers teenagers to thrive and succeed in spite of the obstacles they may encounter. Through open communication, education, and empathy, we can help teenagers develop the skills and resilience necessary to navigate the complexities of the modern world and build a brighter future for themselves and future generations.

- Empowering young people to advocate for change and create impact

Young people today are facing a world full of challenges and uncertainties. From climate change to social injustice, the issues facing our world are complex and daunting. However, young people are not sitting idly by – they are stepping up and advocating for change in unprecedented ways. Empowering young people to advocate for change and create impact is essential in creating a more just and sustainable world for future generations.

One of the key ways to empower young people to advocate for change is to provide them with the knowledge and skills they need to understand the issues they are passionate about. Education is key in this regard – young people need to be informed about the social, political, and environmental issues that are affecting our world today. By equipping them with this knowledge, we are empowering them to make informed decisions and take action to address these issues.

In addition to education, young people also need to develop the skills needed to effectively advocate for change. This includes skills such as public speaking, networking, and strategic communication. By providing young people with opportunities to develop these skills, we are empowering them to effectively communicate their message and mobilize others to take action.

Another important aspect of empowering young people to advocate for change is providing them with opportunities to get involved in their communities and make a difference. This could include volunteering with local organizations, participating in youth-led advocacy campaigns, or even starting their own initiatives. By actively engaging with their communities, young people can see firsthand the impact that their efforts can have and gain valuable experience in creating change.

Furthermore, it is important to create spaces for young people to come together and collaborate on advocacy efforts. By building networks and partnerships with other young advocates, young people can amplify their voices and create a collective impact that is greater than the sum of its parts. This sense of solidarity and collaboration can be a powerful motivation for young people to continue advocating for change and making a difference in the world.

Ultimately, empowering young people to advocate for change is about giving them the tools, resources, and opportunities they need to make a difference. By providing them with the knowledge, skills, and support they need, we are investing in a brighter future for all. Young people are the leaders of tomorrow, and by empowering them to advocate for change, we are helping to create a more just, sustainable, and equitable world for future generations.

Let us continue to support and empower young people in their efforts to create positive change and make a difference in the world.

- Creating a supportive and inclusive society for all youth

Creating a supportive and inclusive society for all youth is a crucial goal that requires a collaborative effort from various stakeholders, including educators, parents, policymakers, and community members. It is essential to recognize the unique challenges faced by young people from diverse backgrounds and to implement strategies that promote their well-being and social inclusion. By fostering a sense of belonging and providing resources and opportunities for growth, we can empower youth to reach their full potential and contribute positively to society.

One key aspect of creating a supportive and inclusive society for youth is ensuring access to quality education. Education plays a pivotal role in shaping the lives of young people and equipping them with the skills and knowledge needed to succeed in a rapidly changing world. It is important to tailor educational programs to meet the diverse needs of students and provide support for those who may face barriers to learning. By promoting inclusive educational practices and fostering a culture of respect and understanding, we can help all youth thrive academically and socially.

In addition to education, it is essential to address the social and emotional well-being of young people. Many youth face mental health challenges, peer pressure, bullying, and other forms of adversity that can impact their overall well-being. By promoting mental health awareness and providing access to support services, we can create a safe and nurturing environment for youth to seek help and build resilience. It is important for adults to listen to the concerns of young people and validate their experiences, while also providing guidance and resources to help them navigate difficult situations.

Another crucial component of creating a supportive and inclusive society for all youth is promoting diversity and equity. It is essential to recognize and celebrate the unique backgrounds, identities, and experiences of young people from diverse communities. By promoting diversity in schools, communities, and workplaces, we can create a more inclusive and welcoming environment for all youth. It is important to address systemic barriers to equity and advocate for social justice to ensure that all young people have the opportunity to thrive and succeed.

In order to create a supportive and inclusive society for all youth, it is important to engage with young people as partners in the process. Youth voice and leadership are essential in shaping policies and programs that impact their lives. It is important to listen to the perspectives and ideas of young people, involve them in decision-making processes, and empower them to be agents of change in their communities. By valuing and respecting the voices of young people, we can create a more inclusive and equitable society that benefits everyone. By prioritizing access to quality education, promoting social and emotional well-being, celebrating diversity and equity, and engaging with young people as partners, we can create a more inclusive and welcoming environment for all youth to thrive. It is important to recognize the unique challenges faced by young people and to implement strategies that promote their well-being and social inclusion. By working together, we can build a society where all youth have the opportunity to reach their full potential and contribute positively to the world.

Chapter 20: Conclusion

- SUMMARY OF KEY TAKEAWAYS from the book

The book "Leaders Eat Last" by Simon Sinek explores the concept of leadership and how it can impact organizational culture. Sinek argues that great leaders prioritize the well-being of their team members above all else, emphasizing the importance of creating a sense of safety and trust within the workplace. He uses real-world examples to illustrate how leaders who put their employees first are ultimately more successful in the long run.

One key takeaway from the book is the idea that leaders should act as protectors of their team members. This means going above and beyond to ensure that employees feel safe, both physically and emotionally, while at work. By creating a culture of trust and support, leaders can empower their team members to take risks and contribute their best work. This not only leads to higher morale and retention rates but also fosters a sense of loyalty and commitment among employees.

Another important concept discussed in the book is the role of empathy in leadership. Sinek emphasizes the importance of truly understanding and caring for the people you lead. By taking the time to listen to their concerns and needs, leaders can build stronger relationships with their team members and create a more positive work environment. This can lead to increased collaboration and innovation, as employees feel more comfortable sharing their ideas and working together towards a common goal.

Additionally, "Leaders Eat Last" highlights the impact that a strong sense of purpose can have on an organization. Sinek argues that successful leaders are able to inspire their team members by clearly communicating the company's mission and values. By aligning individual goals with the larger purpose of the organization, leaders can motivate employees to work towards a shared vision, leading to increased engagement and job satisfaction. By prioritizing the well-being of their team members, practicing empathy, and fostering a sense of purpose, leaders can create a positive and productive work environment that benefits both employees and the organization as a whole. This book serves as a reminder that great leadership is not about power or authority, but rather about serving and supporting those around you.

- The importance of continued support and understanding for teenagers

Teenagers are often seen as a demographic that is misunderstood and undervalued in society. They are at a pivotal stage in their lives where they are navigating the complexities of adolescence and the transition into adulthood. This period of development can be challenging, as teenagers are faced with a myriad of physical, emotional, and social changes. It is crucial that we, as a society, provide continued support and understanding for teenagers during this formative time in their lives.

One of the key reasons why continued support and understanding is vital for teenagers is the impact it can have on their mental health. Teenagers are particularly vulnerable to mental health issues such as anxiety, depression, and eating disorders. These issues can be exacerbated by factors such as academic pressure, social media, and peer relationships. By providing teenagers with the support and understanding they need, we can help to alleviate these stressors and promote positive mental health outcomes. Additionally, research has shown that teenagers who have a strong support system in place are more resilient in the face of adversity and better equipped to cope with challenges.

Furthermore, continued support and understanding for teenagers can also have a positive impact on their academic success. Adolescence is a time when teenagers are under increasing pressure to excel in their studies and prepare for higher education or the workforce. However, many teenagers may struggle with academic pressures, learning disabilities, or lack of resources. By providing ongoing support and understanding, we can help teenagers to overcome these obstacles and reach their full potential. This can include access to tutoring, mentorship programs, and resources for students with learning differences.

When teenagers feel supported and understood in their academic pursuits, they are more likely to excel in school and achieve their goals.

In addition to mental health and academic success, continued support and understanding for teenagers can also have a positive impact on their social and emotional development. Teenagers are at a stage in their lives where they are forming their identity, developing their interpersonal skills, and learning how to navigate relationships with their peers and adults. By providing a safe and supportive environment for teenagers to explore these aspects of themselves, we can help them to build resilience, self-confidence, and empathy. This can lead to healthier relationships, increased self-esteem, and a sense of belonging in their community.

It is important to recognize that teenagers are not just going through a phase, but are individuals with unique talents, interests, and experiences. By providing continued support and understanding for teenagers, we can help them to discover their strengths, passions, and values. This can empower teenagers to pursue their goals, make informed decisions, and contribute positively to society. By fostering a culture of support and understanding for teenagers, we can create a more inclusive and nurturing environment that allows them to thrive and reach their full potential. By recognizing the challenges that teenagers face during adolescence and providing them with the resources, guidance, and empathy they need, we can help them to overcome obstacles, build resilience, and achieve success in all areas of their lives. Teenagers are the future of our society, and it is essential that we invest in their well-being and development. By offering continued support and understanding to teenagers, we can create a brighter and more inclusive future for all.

- Encouragement for parents, educators, and communities to prioritize adolescent well-being

Adolescence is a critical period in a person's life where they transition from childhood to adulthood, and it is essential for parents, educators, and communities to prioritize the well-being of adolescents during this stage. Adolescents are navigating a range of physical, emotional, and social changes, which can be overwhelming and challenging. By prioritizing their well-being, we can help them build the necessary skills and resilience to thrive in adulthood.

Parents play a crucial role in supporting the well-being of adolescents. It is important for parents to create a nurturing and supportive environment where adolescents feel safe and comfortable expressing their thoughts and feelings. By listening to their concerns without judgment and providing guidance and support, parents can help adolescents navigate the challenges they face. Additionally, parents should prioritize open communication with their adolescents, as this can help build trust and strengthen their relationship. By being actively involved in their adolescent's life and showing them love and support, parents can promote their well-being and overall development.

Educators also play a vital role in prioritizing adolescent well-being. Schools should provide a safe and inclusive environment where adolescents can learn and grow. In addition to academic support, schools should also offer resources and programs that focus on mental health and emotional well-being. Educators should be trained to recognize the signs of distress in adolescents and provide appropriate support and guidance. By creating a positive and supportive school culture, educators can help adolescents feel valued and supported, which can have a positive impact on their overall well-being.

Communities can also contribute to prioritizing adolescent well-being. Community organizations and resources should be readily available to support adolescents and their families. By providing access to mental health services, recreational activities, and other support programs, communities can help adolescents build resilience and develop healthy coping mechanisms. In addition, communities should work together to create a supportive and inclusive environment that promotes the well-being of all adolescents. By fostering community connections and promoting positive social norms, communities can help adolescents feel connected and supported, which can improve their overall well-being. Parents, educators, and communities all play a critical role in supporting the well-being of adolescents and helping them navigate the challenges they face during this important stage of life. By creating nurturing and supportive environments, providing resources and programs that focus on mental health, and fostering community connections, we can help adolescents build the skills and resilience they need to thrive in adulthood. By working together to prioritize adolescent well-being, we can create a brighter future for our young people and our communities as a whole.